I Asked the Blue Heron

Mary Anne,

Good luck with the

BY LISBETH COIMAN

One Woman Show.

Lisbeth Coiman

First Edition.

ISBN-13: 978-0-9990812-0-4

To

Zoë Graves, in gratitude.

and

to my children, with love.

Author Notes

1. Reality is a relative concept, even more so for the mentally ill. The story you are about to read depicts actual events as seen through my eyes, the eyes of a woman afflicted by a mental disorder.

2. Some people's names have been changed to protect their privacy.

3. The explicit and graphic content of this story may shock, offend, or trigger some readers.

4. The majestic Great Blue Heron, or Gran Garza Azul, lives primarily in North America, as far as Alaska and Canada, where the Migratory Bird Treaty Act protects it. But in winter, it can fly south to Venezuela's coast.

Source: https://www.allaboutbirds.org/guide/Great_Blue_Heron/lifehistory

Acknowledgements

My deepest gratitude goes to the following individuals:

To my husband and children, for enduring the ups and downs of my mental condition with loving care and support.

To Zoë Graves, for being an enlightened witness in my life.

To my teachers from Escuela Estatal Simón Rodríguez in Guarenas, Venezuela: Alicia, Olga, Elizabeth, Izmenia, Josefa, Janette, and Peralta, for providing safe space and nurturing my innocent child mind. To all my teachers thereafter, for nurturing my intellect and soul.

To Doctor Hamilton, for encouraging me to write this story and for helping me deal with the painful memories. To Dr. Doyle, Dr. Silver, and Diane Duffy, for taking care of me during the worst crisis of my life. To Irene Gutierrez, for her loving and caring approach to mental health professional practice. To Marianela Manzanares for her unconditional support and humorous approach to mental health.

To Theo Pauline Nestor and Ariel Gore for guiding my writing process and opening their writing communities to me. To all the fellow writers in the Literary Kitchen, for critiquing my rough drafts and understanding early on that I write in a second language. Special thanks to Sarah Medina, Elisa Sinnet, Kate Dreyfuss, Bonnie Dittevsen, Jodie Fleming, Diana Kirk, Jenny Forrester, Ann Yarrow, Margaret Elisa Garcia, and Michelle Gonzales, mi hermana Xicana, for having my back. To Suzanne Finnamore, for her encouragement and humor. To the South Bay Writing Group in Redondo Beach: Jenny Chow,

Tracey Dale, Robin Arehart, and Sherry Berkin, for being part of my creative process, and for reading my work week after week.

Special thanks to Ashaki Jackson, for reaching out to me to offer so many hours finding all the holes in the story, and to my editor, Xochitl-Julisa Bermejo for the minute care given to the final draft. Finally, thanks to Ramona Gonzales for looking for typos and spelling before the manuscript went to press.

To all my friends from near and far and not listed here, because they are the family that holds me when I am falling. And to my sister, Rosa Elena Coiman, for finally standing up for me.

Table of Contents

"Migration gives a blank check to put anything you don't feel like addressing in the memory hold. No neighbors can go against the monster narrative of your family." - *Junot Díaz*

"Happy families are all alike; every unhappy family is unhappy in its own way." - *Leo Tolstoy*

Runaway Daughter

I WAS SIXTEEN when my mother chased me with a hammer. I locked myself in the bathroom. When she went to look for the key, I ran out through the door to the police station about a mile down the hill from my house. The officer knew my father and persuaded me to go back home. "I am going to call Coiman. I'm sure your family can work this out," he said as he dialed my home number. "The only place you can go to is a correctional facility where there will be no distinction between a young woman running away from her angry mother and a young criminal." He handed me back to my father. After all, this was Venezuela in the late 70s.

The nationalization of the oil industry in the mid 70s brought wealth and progress to the once rural nation. Construction of highways and block buildings exploded alongside employment opportunities. My mother joined thousands of other workers in the long commute to Caracas everyday, leaving her seven children to take care of each other. Always energized, she woke up at four a.m., cooked breakfast and lunch for all, dressed up, and went to work.

A woman of simple taste, my mother wore loose blouses and comfortable pants that accentuated her voluminous behind. She used minimal make up and brushed her hair in waves with a white plastic brush, which became elusive when she ran around the house tending to the arepas in the oven and getting ready for work. In the stressful mornings, a scream was frequently heard: "¿Dónde coño e'madre está mi cepillo?"

She came back after dark, tired from the long bus ride, but with enough stamina left to discipline her children and get ready for the next day, barking instructions while setting up a pressure pot with black beans on the stove and a load of laundry in the washer.

*

AT 18, I left again after a fight over dirty dishes and chores. It was a Sunday. I had returned from a field trip with my dance group in college, a full day of folk music and traditions in Barlovento. A pile of dishes was waiting for me. I protested. In her tank top and shorts, she had been busy working hard to complete all the domestic chores she didn't have time to do during her workweek.

"But there are other people in this house," I protested. "Mi papá and my brothers could help clean." In our family, cleaning duties, laundry, cooking, and dishes were a woman's job, even if that woman had to commute 60 miles by connecting buses to go to work 40 hours a week, or hitchhike to go to college. She started yelling insults at me: "Esta mujer floja nació pa' puta." She made a racket smashing dishes against pans and cutlery. As usual, her temper escalated from a spark. Suddenly, she grabbed a butcher knife from the sink and swatted at me. I ran and put the dining table between us. She darted from one side of the table to the other, unable to reach me. Then, she lifted her right hand over her head and threw the knife at me like a baseball. The knife landed on the right edge of my glasses' frame and grazed my temple, where it made a small cut. Blood dripped down on my shirt.

Meanwhile, my father walked around, unsuccessfully trying to control her. "Quédate tranquila, chica," he said.

But she was already beyond calming down. Her explosive and violent anger, like a pressure pot, needed to be completely released before it came to a stop. When she noticed the blood on my shirt, she went to my bedroom. One by one, she took the drawers from the dresser, walking with each one over her head to the front of the house. She threw them out the front door with the same strength a construction worker would use to slam a sack of cement to the ground, all amid profanities and insults.

"If you don't like my government, take exile," she said.

I stepped over the scattered drawers. Sobbing loudly, I bent over to pick up a toothbrush and a hundred bolívares, and left.

Already in my third semester in college, I spent the night at a friend's apartment. The next evening I made my bed on a church bench. Monday, I skipped school but went directly to my part time job and explained my situation to the secretary, who took me into her apartment in the same building as our office. I asked this woman to call me only by my first name, Lisbeth. Before that, I went by my middle name, Carolina.

My mother somehow managed to find me, but she asked for Carolina over the phone, and the woman answered, "There is no Carolina here. You must have the wrong phone number."

I moved a few more times and eventually left the part time job to take a full time position as a bilingual receptionist at Heinz Foods in Caracas. Somewhat settled, I enrolled in a community college to study marketing.

Two years later, I was pregnant and unwed, but how I reach that point is a whole other story.

*

THE YOUNG, female doctor sat on a wheeled stool and reached behind her for a focus lamp. She then positioned the lamp so that she could see clearly between my legs. "When did the bleeding start? she asked.

"About a week ago," I said.

"Does it hurt?"

"Yes, like cramps."

She placed my ultrasound image on her desk. "Placenta previa," she said. "This is a high-risk pregnancy. You need to be on bed rest until you come to term. Let somebody take care of you."

"I can't," I said wiping my tears.

"Do you have anywhere to go? Parents, a godmother, anyone?" The doctor asked while looking down at her clipboard. She then grabbed her long hair, twisted it several times, and pinned it up with her pencil.

Predicting complications and long-term absences, the Heinz company prepared an almost irresistible severance package if I resigned: my salary until three months after giving birth, with paid vacation, and all perks doubled. I used the money as the down payment for a subsidized apartment in a new subdivision under construction in Guatire, the neighbor city of Guarenas, suburbs to the east of Caracas.

The day I went home – pregnant, sick, and unemployed – my mother waited for me at her door. Rows of duplex houses with pathways formed a square around a green community space. She announced to the entire neighborhood, "The lost bird comes back to her nest." The women sitting on their porches turned their heads in my direction, attentive to gossip material.

My parents rejoiced with the expectation of a new baby in the family. My mother emphasized my being sick. I was not supposed to lift any weight, but was expected to help with small house chores, like washing the dishes. My father wanted a financial contribution since I soon would be adding another mouth to feed. They took turns reminding me of their generosity.

"Tú no quieres a ese bebé, por eso es que se te sale la placenta," my mother mentioned one day while she crocheted tiny booties as keepsakes for the baby's visitors.

I cried and wandered around the house in a haze, unable to visualize a loving family. In my moments of wellness, I shopped for tiny baby clothes, which I folded neatly. I held them to my face to breathe in the sweet smell.

*

THE NEIGHBOR'S MANGO tree stood about 40 feet tall and 15 feet wide. Its branches hung over the concrete wall, separating the two backyards. One of the tree limbs lay over the top of the water tank, at the bottom end of our backyard. An asbestos panel protected the water tank from debris and animals. To fill the tank with the hose of the cistern truck, we had to slide the asbestos panel, which was covered with mangoes and dead leaves.

Too heavy to climb the ladder to the top of the tank, I waited for the cistern truck men to come inside the house and cross the living room with their massive hose so they could get through to the backyard. I stopped them and gave them a bucket. "Can you fill this with mangoes while you are up there?"

I sweltered, sitting on the stairs in the afternoon heat. I bit the mango skin with a hunger that couldn't be nourished, smearing my face and clothes with their sweet yellow mess, thinking of ways to raise the baby. The baby grew inside me, in my parents' house, under the shade of our neighbor's tree, while I fed on mangoes and worried about an uncertain future.

*

TRYING TO BE A mom felt like a gargantuan task and an obsession. I couldn't take my eyes off of his beautiful face. He cried in long deafening shrills. Nothing would satisfy him but the milk of my breasts. I was overcome with sweetness and tenderness when his nose and mouth looked for my nipple in desperate moves of his little bushy head like a puppy, all instinct.

Then he would suck on that nipple and finally give in to sleep, cuddled in my arms, his lips still moving. We enjoyed this bliss when we were alone. I sat in the rocking chair in front of the TV, immersed in the beauty of the moment.

The first sight of his tiny teeth was a curiosity. Every family member came and peeked into the little mouth of the two-month old to see the white serrated line in his lower gum. I had to sit still, doing my best not to disturb him while feeding, rocking carefully, with imperceptible movements of the chair until we both fell asleep in the heat of the evening.

One day after we had dozed off, my mother arrived home from work at around seven. "Ramón," she called out.

The baby woke up, startled. He clamped his new teeth on me and turned his little head looking for my mother's voice.

I grimaced in pain; she smiled. Ramón sucked blood and milk from my breast. Feeding my baby became another form of torture under my mother's sadistic control. Yet it was my breast, not hers, that he wanted.

When my son was four months old, I closed on the apartment in Guatire and moved in with the baby's biological father. A few weeks and a couple of beatings later, I put the apartment up for rent and moved back in with my parents.

*

MY MIND WAS already fragmented, but the smiling woman standing in front of me couldn't have seen that. I answered the touch-tone phone, holding it between my ear and my neck, signaling the white lady and her companions to give me a minute with the other hand. I quickly typed a reservation on the screen of my IBM. "Aló, Vista Club y Pisos Ejecutivos. How may I serve you?" The chic lobby of the Caracas Hilton Hotel hummed with visitors on a sunny morning in February. It was one of the two best hotels in the nation, if not the best.

I was a fast typist, with chirpy phone skills, who could make reservations in several languages and smile enough to pass as agreeable. Although I could not patronize restaurants, I could make sound dining recommendations, in English or German, albeit halted, with a big, attractive smile and a batting of lashes.

I finished the reservation and hung up. "I apologize for making you wait. How can I help you?"

The middle-aged white woman dressed in a pastel housedress with a small purse slung across her body spoke for the group. Her companions carried maps, guidebooks and cameras.

"We're staying a few days in Venezuela. Could you recommend things to do?" Her lively eyes accentuated the radiant smile on her face framed by dark brown, short hair.

"I'm Lisbeth, nice to meet you."

She extended her hand and a bright smile to me, "Zoë. These are Karen and Ellie."

"How would you like to lie on a beach by the Caribbean Sea?" I suggested.

They commented among each other before saying a loud, "Yes."

"Well, please sit down," I said. "This is going to take a few minutes." I arranged a hotel in Juan Griego (a stunning beach, which houses the old La Galera Fortress, a small fort overlooking the ocean and a favorite spot to catch the sunset on Margarita Island), a return flight to Maiquetía, and the connection to New York.

"You'll love Juan Griego and Margarita Island as a whole, with its turquoise Caribbean beaches. Watch your belongings and enjoy your vacation. Anything else I can do for you?" I said after I finished explaining the arrangements for the trip.

"Could you also make a reservation for a city tour of Caracas?"

"I can do that myself," I said, leaning forward and lowering my voice. "My shift ends at two. We can meet at half past two on the street at the other side of the hotel." It was a good way to earn some extra cash, better than hoping for tips.

"You'll be tired by then," Zoë said.

"I don't have a reason to rush back home after my shift today. My mother took my baby to the beach for the long weekend. I have a few days off from home. It'll be nice for me to go out with friendly people."

*

WITH MY SON away on vacation, I enjoyed a temporary sense of peace. I slipped on running shoes, a pair of jeans, and a t-shirt when my shift ended. I met Zoë on the ample sidewalk of Avenida Mexico, adjacent to the hotel. It was Carnaval, and we could see children in costumes walking around the city – an adorable batman, a sweet vampire, a cute Dalmatian toddler on a leash. The warm early March air with its sunny skies begged me to go to the beach. Instead, I took the tourists downtown in a cab.

We strolled the cobblestone streets where Simón Bolivar, our founding father, had been born. We sat down in the Plaza Bolivar, near the equestrian statue, to watch the sloths come down from the centuries old Samanes (Albizia) trees and feed from the hands of school children. I showed Zoë and her friends downtown Caracas with its charming mix of Spanish Colonial and 19th century French architecture.

Zoë asked questions while snapping pictures of children wherever we walked around. I learned that she lived in Manhattan where she worked for a children's theater company. She spoke excitedly about the costumes, songs, and makeup her group was preparing for an upcoming production. Already in her early forties, Zoë appeared to me as a city woman full of confidence and charisma. When we stopped to eat some shaved ice or chicha criolla, she made eye contact with the vendor, tried saying gracias with a broad smile, and tipped generously.

After sightseeing Caracas, and when I felt my brain was about to explode from remembering so many historical facts and dates, I suggested taking the cable car to the top of El Avila, the impressive mountain that separates the city from the Caribbean Sea and dominates the small valley-city landscape. In the middle of the dry season, the majestic mountain was dressed in red with the bloom of the rubrum, a tall burgundy grass that covers the south facing hills. At sunset, the light touched the fussy plumes and gave a unique show of light and color, that would decades later bring tears to the eyes of the diaspora when remembered from the distance of the exile.

Once at the top, we walked around the abandoned Humboldt Hotel. Night had fallen already, so we couldn't see the ocean or the north slope of the mountain. Rather, we sat by the rock wall and talked in low voices about Venezuela, and their lives in New York. When it was time to go back, we joined hundreds of other passengers queuing to board the cable car back to the city.

In that slow waiting line, Zoë saw through me.

"You should come with us to Juan Griego," she said.

"I can't. I'm not allowed."

"Excuse me?" she said with a slight frown. "Because of your job?"

"No. Not my job. My mother. She would not allow me to go with you."

"How old are you, Lisbeth?"

I wished we were back in downtown. I lost command of the conversation, wanting to be under the Samanes' shade again, relaxed in all of my historical knowledge. My face flushed.

"I'm 23."

"You are a mother, a heck of a tour guide, an efficient hostess. And you don't have permission to go to the beach?" She was no longer smiling.

My voice stuttered in the evening.

"My mother takes care of my son only if I work, but I'm not allowed to go out, date or anything. She keeps a close eye on me."

Zoë took a step closer to me, lowered her voice, and continued digging. "But she is on a beach, hundreds of miles away. You have the weekend off. She wouldn't even know."

"She'd know. She has spies all over," I said.

Zoë squinted at me.

We were not speaking comfortably anymore. I noticed the dark eyes above her long nose. She looked at me with empathy. She was old enough to be my mother, probably in her mid forties. I was only 23. Short curls framed my slim face. She must have noticed the fear in my round, dark eyes, but I didn't want to deal with this in front of a group of tourists. People began glancing in our direction.

The line didn't move and the night was closing in around us. "What's the worst thing that will happen, anyway? She will get mad and she will have to get happy again."

"She'll beat me."

She pressed, "It's just that you're twenty-three, and I can't wrap my head around it."

"My brothers would also beat me." I lost control of my now shrill voice and leaned into the confession, denouncing my family to strangers.

"Lisbeth. Look at me, honey. You need to leave that house soon. This is very important. You need to take your child and leave that house for good."

For the first time somebody validated my feelings; somebody said there was something wrong in my life. She explained to me that raising my son in that environment would only perpetuate a line of abuse that would extend for generations. "Is that what you want for your child?"

I knew it all along, but nobody around me ever said anything wrong about mothers. Mothers were Biblical haloed nurturers, carrying their children while smiling sublimely.

The large cable car cabin rocked with our weight as we stepped in late that night. I sat and found comfort staring into the lights while Zoë and her friends chatted about the experiences of the day. The city was asleep by the time we arrived back.

We headed to an arepera for a light midnight dinner in a restaurant filled with drunken clients lined up in the wee hours. I gave the New York tourists the words they needed to order their food, and they shouted, trying unsuccessfully to roll their "Rs."

"Reina pepeada!" "Queso guaya!" "Batidos!"

They chatted about what the US equivalent of Caracas would be.

"Elizabeth, New Jersey," Zoë offered.

"No, it's like New York," I said.

They let out a collective chuckle.

Weeks after their departure, I received a small package in the mail. It contained a postcard with a command, a twenty-dollar bill, and a white t-shirt with green stripes that I had eyed on our visit to Sabana Grande.

> We had such a good time in Juan Griego. We missed you! You are an excellent tour guide. Thank you!
>
> You must leave your parents home as soon as possible. You can't raise your child in that environment. Mr. Jackson will help you start your moving away fund.
>
> Write back soon.
>
> Love, Zoë

Hechiceros

"PÉINATE ESOS CHICHARRONES. Esta muchacha el carajo!" My mother shouted as I headed out the door.

I was frustrated with my mother's constant complaints about my nappy hair. When I was younger, she took me often to the hairdresser to cut my hair short, or to straighten it.

I wasn't completely sure what I wanted to do with my hair until I entered the salon. In the background Madonna sang "Borderline" through a boom box on the floor next to the hairdresser's chair. I asked the young hairdresser if she would shave my head.

"I do whatever people pay me to do," said the hairdresser as she buzzed her electric razor close to my ears.

"*Keep pushing me,*" Madonna repeated as the humming of the clipper uncovered a segment of my scalp, and long frizzy curls fell on the floor.

The shaved head did not go unnoticed at the Hilton, where my honeymoon phase ended abruptly. It was an uphill battle with the new boss, coworkers, and administration. It's hard to say from this distance if I wouldn't have been fired before I quit.

*

WITH MY NEWFOUND free time and a sprout of creativity, I bought some fabric and fashioned a pair of faded baggy pants. I took a sleeveless white t-shirt and decorated it with old, discarded buttons. That was my new outfit; I wore it everywhere I went.

It was near Easter, which in Venezuela means another ten-day vacation, so I took my little son to the beach. In the afternoons, Ramón and I built sand castles and played in the shallow water, where the waves broke and dragged swimmers under. He was my skinny little man with big round, dark eyes like a Japanese anime character. Playing on that beach, he called me tía.

"Soy tu mamá."

"No. Grandma is my mom. She said to call her mamá. You are my auntie."

Zoë's advice to leave the abusive home loomed. How would I make it without help? Who would take care of Ramón while I went to work?

*

I WALKED UP the stairs to the cafeteria of the Asociación Cultural Humboldt (ACH), the Goethe Institute in Caracas. My steps echoed on the hardwood stairs of the modern building located in San Bernardino, a middle class neighborhood in the north central part of the city. I had just enrolled in the next level of German classes and sat down to have a cup of coffee before starting my long commuting trip back home. My white top with buttons glowed against the tan that I brought back from my week in Boca de Uchire.

I spotted Jussef Awad at the bar. He reached for the espresso cup in front of him, brought the cup to his long, aquiline nose, and smelled the fresh brewed coffee. He swirled the tiny cup around a couple of times, looked inside at its contents with deep intent. I observed his thick eyebrows framing sad eyes behind glasses. On this lazy afternoon in mid-April, it seemed that nothing else was more important to him than the bitter taste of coffee and the light coming through the glass wall to his right.

A young engineer working for the country's oil company, Jussef was single and enjoyed the comfortable life of a middle-class professional, with some baggage on his shoulder. Jussef's mother was widowed in her early thirties when Jussef was just 17. While his father was in his deathbed, a skinny Jussef promised to take care of his mother and his siblings.

The attractive young woman and her teenage son with the sad eyes finished growing up together. Jussef became her partner, helping her raise his younger siblings and managing the family's fast-disappearing wealth. He never had a chance to misbehave. By the time we met, the younger siblings were teenagers and giving his mom a lot of grief.

A group of old classmates had introduced me to Jussef a couple of months before while riding the bus after classes. We exchanged phone numbers then, but I didn't call. I also didn't stop thinking about him.

We greeted each other and hugged as if we were old friends. An electric current went from where my breast brushed his chest, to where my cheeks burned against his three-day-old beard, and down to where my thighs met.

My body's reaction to his had been so evident that if he commented on it, I would never be able to say, "You imagined that."

My body said, "This is the man you are looking for." And I felt embarrassed. He kissed me again on the other cheek. This was strange because, affectionate as we Venezuelans are, we don't do the two-cheek-kiss-thing.

He ordered coffee for me, and we talked about our new class schedules, discovering we would be in the same German class.

"What are you doing tonight?" he asked.

"I'm going back home." I played with the curls beginning to grow back on the back of my head as I swam in the lakes of his sad eyes.

"Let's go to the movies," he suggested.

I bit my lower lip with doubt. "I live far away in Guarenas."

"I'll drive you back, don't worry." He dismissed my concern with a gesture of his hand, reassuring me that he had everything under control.

"I need to be home early. I have a baby."

"Are you married?" He looked at me over the rim of his glasses.

"No."

*

NICOLAS CAGE, COVERED in flour and sweat, showed his gloved hand onscreen and declared that his life had been taken away from him. Later, Cage carried Cher to a large bed. She spoke with a great Brooklyn-Italian accent and dressed like a middle-aged New Yorker. Nothing made sense because I was feeling Jussef hard in my hand. He was kissing me all over, and his hands were lost under my sleeveless white top. I felt a button fall between the seats.

I felt disoriented as we walked out of the movie theater. I was high with desire, and burning between my legs. Jussef was still playing with my neck, kissing me softly. "I need to go home," I said.

When we arrived at my house, the neighborhood had long gone to bed. Jussef parked the car, and I talked about my baby. "I don't exist without him. If you are interested in me, you're interested in my son."

His response was a kiss. Did Jussef hear me that night? Another hour passed, during which our hands and arms moved in every direction. Our lips kissed any exposed skin. I could hear the concert of crickets, bats, cats, barking dogs, and the sucking of our lips as we kissed each other to madness.

We were still necking with hunger inside the car when I remembered my mother, how angry she would be because I was late. I wondered how she was going to punish me this time. I leaned on Jussef's ear and said, "Vamonos a Canadá."

"¿A Canadá? ¿Por qué Canadá?" he asked with a chuckle. His thick eyebrows met in the middle.

"Because I hate my mother. But I don't want to talk about that today. I had a wonderful evening."

"I enjoyed it, too. He leaned forward, and his aquiline nose touched mine. "What is this?" He asked.

"I don't know, but I like it. What did you do to me in that theater?"

"It's the moon," he said.

"Hechicero," I teased. "I must go, like right now. Look how late it is."

"I just cast a spell on you," he said, looking intensely into my eyes, overacting to tease me.

I opened the door and stepped out of the car. I closed the door and walked to his side. "Good bye, hechicero," I said, kissing him once more.

Walking the few steps to my front door that night, I searched for the charm I had tucked inside my wallet. A guest at the Hilton had given me a little hand as an amulet, after she overheard me speaking about my broken dreams of earning a PhD and becoming a writer. She said one day I would have a second chance.

The hamsa was of solid silver, about an inch long, with an intricate relief pattern. She said that for Jews, hamsa represents hope, but when received as a gift, it brings good luck. I took it out of my purse in the darkness, held it in my hand, and pressed it against my chest. I said a silent prayer as I entered the house well past my curfew and braced myself for havoc.

*

ZOË AND I KEPT in touch; our letters traveled slowly between NYC and Guarenas. I sent news about my life raising Ramón in Venezuela. She was always surprised at the lack of public agencies that could support mothers. She spoke about shelters for victims of domestic abuse and social services. "Is there anything like a YMCA there?" she asked me once. "They would have at least free day care." Even the concept was foreign to me. While I understood perfectly well what she wanted me to do, I had no easy way to access similar services. There was no adequate and affordable childcare for my infant son. I had nothing to rely on for support if I decided to leave.

Zoë was a Baby Boomer – independent, a traveler who collected friends during her trips. She built her life according to her own rules.

> 6/25/90
>
> I'm working hard to start my own business. That is the main thing going on with me. It means I work all day at my job, and then come home and work all night on jobs for myself. I don't think I'll be able to take any vacation this year because of all the work. I will continue to do this until my own work becomes steady and continuous and I can leave my job… My business is growing, and I hope I'll be able to break away before the end of the year.

We would never meet for coffee after work, or be together for our birthdays, but we did become a constant in each other's lives. Sometimes we were lucky and our letters arrived within three weeks. Sometimes they took several months before making it to my door. It was a halted conversation, but it was profound, meaningful, and heartfelt. This honest, slow paced chat got me closer to her than to any of my female relatives and painted a clear image of the woman I wanted to become.

*

BRIGHT LIGHT ENTERED the living room of my parents' house and spilled onto the rattan sofa where my mother sat. Across from her, my son's biological father leaned forward on a wicker chair. My eyes darted from one face to the other. I couldn't figure out what he was doing there. He only visited my son on rare occasions and never ever provided financial support to raise the child.

"I'll file for custody on charges of negligence," I heard her tell him.

I froze. She wanted my son.

Her parenting of my other siblings was by no means exemplary, but it contrasted sharply with the way she treated me, who grew up without the gentle touch of a loving mother. Despite her dictatorial ways in general, she never reached the level of elaborate abuse, such as filing for custody of my child, against anybody else in our household. To me, she inflicted pain not just in the outburst of anger.

With the scene unfolding in front of my eyes, I could see that my mother was planning to take my son from me, legally. And I wasn't going to allow her. If somebody had cut my vein, I wouldn't have bled a drop. My blood froze, and in that instant, I buried whatever remained of filial love deep inside of me. This woman couldn't be my mother, even though she had given birth to me.

I turned to her and said, "I won't waste my time arguing with you."

I turned to the man with the fiercest look in my eyes and said, "You file for custody, and I'll put you in jail. You know I can." My voice was steady, even unbothered. I proceeded to my bedroom with a firm stride.

Mine had been an unwanted pregnancy, but once Ramón was born, I loved him more than my own life and was ready to die for him. I made the decision in that moment: I would be responsible for my life and my child's. I found my way out.

*

I HAD RENTED out my apartment to pay the mortgage. To leave my mother's house, I had to look for more affordable alternatives. We moved to a room in an apartment on the busy Avenida Fuerzas Armadas, in San José, a low middle-class parish in the north central part of Caracas.

Little Ramón and I shared the apartment with two other women I hardly knew and paid the rent to a landlady who lived in the same building. I dragged myself from the top of the bunk bed and woke up my son who slept underneath. Car lights sparkled in the darkness outside in the city. Ramón, then four, dressed himself while I cooked breakfast. Together we made the beds and brushed our teeth.

Riding the 13 km on the bus from San José in the north to El Valle in the south, I heard rumors of riots. It was only a few miles, but with traffic, it felt like forever. My aunt opened the door of her apartment and took Ramón in. She cared for him during the day for a small fee. She made no comments about what I had heard on the bus.

From there, in the subway to Chacaíto, I asked questions about the riots. "La Guardia está en la calle," a woman told me. A small tank patrolled the street adjacent to the law firm where I worked as an office manager. The three employees surely would come early, I thought. It was payday.

I called the boss and described the situation to him. The boss advised me to wait for the employees, pay them, and make sure the safety box was locked before I left. They didn't show up. The day went by slowly, and all the while, the news played on the office's small radio.

Broadcasters reported that at 4 a.m., the mass of commuters from Guarenas to Caracas discovered gas prices had spiked overnight and bus fares tripled. They showed their discontent by looting and destroying buses, businesses, and anything in between. The looting soon spread like a grass fire across all the major cities of the country. By 7 a.m., television cameras brought images of social unrest in Caracas, Barquisimeto, Valencia, and Cumaná. It was apparent in those first images that the police and the National Guard had done nothing to stop the angry masses.

By 3 p.m., I decided to get to my son as soon as possible.

All public transportation had ceased. I walked and hitchhiked on the back of motorbikes across the city, desperate to reach my aunt's apartment. My pantyhose were ripped, and one shoe had lost its heel. I reached El Valle by six in the evening. Looting was on its way. In the apartment, Ramón was curled under a bed.

Jussef called. "I got to get you out of there."

I insisted it was difficult. The looters had blocked the Intercomunal del Valle, the main avenue in that part of the city, with burning tires; there wasn't any through traffic. My aunt suggested I leave the child there and have my father pick him up the next day and get him to Guarenas, where he would be safe while I stayed with Jussef in his apartment. I still needed to work. It was the best for Ramón.

Well past bedtime, Jussef picked me up. I spent the night at his apartment. The next day, I decided to make my way back to my place to evaluate the situation. The National Guard was out and shooting at people in my neighborhood. I hitchhiked again from Avenida Andrés Bello to Avenida

Fuerzas Armadas, maybe 5 kilometers. This time I carried a bandana drenched in vinegar with me because the city air reeked with tear gas. I headed north at the corner of Socarrás. On the bridge over Avenida Panteón, a dead man lay facedown on a puddle of blood, a carton of milk in his hand. I stepped around him and continued north on the famous avenue's ample mosaic sidewalk.

Two blocks before my destination, I heard gunshots. The National Guard aimed their guns at a supermarket on the opposite side of the avenue. Like ants, people went in and out of the supermarket, carrying the weight of their loot. A man fell with a sack of flour on his back. I ran to my apartment building door and stepped through as tear gas stung my eyes. Inside the apartment, my roommates laughed and retold the tales of their looting experiences. I was appalled. We weren't desperate or hungry.

I didn't confront them or express my opinion about the looting. Venezuela was a country of abundance then. I made small talk about what I had seen in the city. I told them I'd been wearing the same clothes for 24 hours, and that the tear gas had gotten to me. I needed to shower more than anything, and I needed to pack. "I'll come back when I can," I said. And went back to Jussef's place.

The truth is that I saw myself as above them. I wasn't that type of person. We shared an apartment, but I wouldn't loot; I didn't find it necessary or justifiable. I resented them, in their camaraderie, but also in their lack of civic responsibility.

The gas prices stayed high, and the country seemed to dive deeper into its corrupt ways.

"Is this war?" Ramón asked when we were finally able to meet again at the end of the week at my mother's house in Guarenas.

"I don't know. It's the end of Carnaval, and people are taking off their masks." I kissed his forehead, "That's all, fallen masks."

*

OUR LIVING ARRANGEMENTS changed. Jussef had plans to go to the United States in the summertime to do graduate work. He asked me to stay in his apartment with him until he moved north, but he wasn't ready to have a child in his life. After he left, I could bring Ramón and live rent-free until he came back two years later.

I breathed in deeply and closed my eyes to visualize a serene life for my son and me. Jussef had offered a good deal, but it meant leaving Ramón with my parents for four months. I considered my odds, tossing and turning in bed at night.

It would take my mother more than four months to build up a case against me if she insisted on taking full custody of Ramón. A social worker would have a hard time finding any evidence of neglect because I could easily prove to the world without much effort that I was a hardworking single mother. I provided consistently for my son and helped my parents financially, even if they were not interested in acknowledging that publicly.

Meanwhile, I could use those four months to save money and prepare for my son to live with me permanently. While he was with my parents, I could find affordable day care and make arrangements so that I could work even when he had days off, which was a major issue because when school was out, I struggled to find care for him. One thing was sure: I knew that Ramón was beloved, and well taken care of in my parents' house.

I took the risk.

I moved from San José to Jussef's apartment on Avenida Andrés Bello by mid-March, with the agreement that Jussef would leave for the United States in June. As part of the plan, I would sell my apartment in Guatire and use the money to finish college.

During the week, I was happy to be with Jussef and away from my family. We would meet after work for a beer in Sabana Grande or go to the movies. We felt free to have spontaneous sex.

I called Ramón every day at my parents' house, took care of all his expenses, and on Friday afternoons, I picked him up to spend the weekend with Jussef and me. When I returned him to Guarenas on Sunday afternoons, I could count on drama.

"Esta bolloloco dejo al hijo por un macho," my mother said.

"Yo no lo abandoné. Es sólo por unos meses. Por favor tengan paciencia," I pleaded.

I tried my best to save money, to show that I was determined to bring Ramón with me, but it didn't work. Every Sunday afternoon, the same storm of insults. My head hurt as if someone had poked a screwdriver in the back of my eyes. I rode the bus back to the city with my helplessness and guilt.

One Sunday, my father's brother and my mother's younger sister visited my parents. When it was time to leave, my uncle offered to drive us back to the city. We all hopped in his car: my aunt, her two daughters, my uncle, and me. We sat closely, arms touching each other with the windows open for air. My uncle rode slowly uphill on the Petare-Guarenas Highway.

My aunt broke the silence. "You abandoned your child for a man."

Her accusation fell hard on my stomach. I felt ambushed. My voice rose to a shrill, "I have not abandoned him!"

"That's what you say now, but we all know that you'll leave the child with your parents. You never wanted to have that child anyway."

I could hear my mother's words coming from my aunt's mouth. She had repeated the statement so many times, as if an unplanned pregnancy was a crime. Blessed is the woman who desires every child she conceives, and conceives every child she desires.

"It's only temporary. I talked with mi mamá and mi papá about it already." I cried while stretching my neck out the window, gasping for air. Then I turned to her, "I don't understand. Mi mamá said she would die because I took the baby away. Now the baby is with her, but you are accusing me of abandoning him."

"That man will never love your child," she said.

"Uncle, can you stop the car now, please? Right now! I want to stop right here. I will find my way home, don't worry." I stepped out of the car and hitchhiked back to my parents' home. Once more, I tried to explain that it was only a temporary arrangement. In June, Ramón would move in with me. But it was useless.

"You'll never be happy," my mother cursed.

I traveled back to Jussef's place in tears, with an excruciating headache. I couldn't force Jussef to accept living with a child, and I couldn't just keep moving from one place to another. In those days, misery caused me to vomit daily. I became so slim that those who knew me were concerned about my health. I pressed on working hard while Jussef prepared for his upcoming trip. I counted down the days until Ramón could live with me.

Guacamayas[1] *and Guacharacas*[2]

ZOË WAS TRAVELING AROUND the world. She slowly transitioned from her theater company to her own business, Creative Medical Communications. In her letters, she seemed well in control of her life although love eluded her. Men who were drawn to her never remained close; they left her in tears after moving on to better jobs or better situations in life. While she bonded with people in every city she visited, she lacked the same kind of success with the men in her life. Yet her altruism served everyone – the men who left and the people she befriended in her travels. She offered a helping hand, bringing the best out in the people she met, helping them achieve goals they didn't even allow themselves to dream. Zoë had a gift for improving people's lives.

She overwhelmed me with advice despite our letters slowly crawling from continent to continent. My memory of her face faded. I no longer remembered her voice or her accent, but she grew in my mind as an ideal. We were safe from the everyday friction that sometimes arises between women who are close friends.

Zoë was happy that I had finally moved out and warned me about going back whenever I complained about my living arrangements. I wanted Ramón

[1] *Macaws*
[2] *Rufous-vented chachalaca bird*

with me, but I couldn't force Jussef into a situation for which he wasn't ready. "He has offered a viable solution; take it and be patient," she wrote.

Sometimes her letters spoke of her love of children, how much she wanted to have one of her own.

> 6/2/92
>
> Guess where I am? In Portland with my friend Lisa, and her brand new baby! She called me the morning of June 1 to tell me her water had broken. I jumped on the next plane out, and arrived just in time for the deliver. We call him Luke. He is handsome, with dark eyes, a tiny nose and brown, curly hair. He is perfect and a pleasure to be around. I know what you are thinking, when am I going to adopt a baby? It feels I wouldn't want to do it alone although I know I could if necessary. I don't know at this point who that someone would be.

*

WHEN JUSSEF LEFT in June for Cincinnati, I felt as if the skin had been pulled off of my arm. It ached to think of him away. I had never experienced this kind of love – a lover who didn't hurt, who cared for me, who was concerned for me and my son's wellbeing despite the fact that he wouldn't live with the child yet. He called on Sunday afternoons – our weekly phone dates. We wrote long loving letters about our lives, and how we spent the days, what we ate for dinner, when we thought about each other, the people we met, the things we did, and the mutual longing for each other's bodies. He knew how to keep the fire going at a distance. I slept with his letters tucked under my pillow.

> 11/1/89

¿Qué dudas son estas? No, mon amour, no dudes jamás de mi amor. Ni por un instante. Te quiero, mon amour. ¿Claro? Por supuesto me estoy jugando muchas cosas en está decisión de venirme a estudiar a Cincinnati. Entre otras cosas está nuestra relación – nada más y nada menos – Pero lo hago con la convicción – casi con la certeza – que si logramos lo que estamos buscando y que si la relación sobrevive todas estas dificultades entonces la misma saldrá SUPER FORTALECIDA. Es una prueba dura, durísima, pero vital, mon amour.

9/16/89

TE QUIERO. TE AMO. Cada minuto que pasa solo me lo confirma. Estas muy sembrada dentro de mi. No eres fácil de arrancar, ni tampoco es mi intención. Cada vez que comparto con otras personas también me confirman ese sentimiento. Solo o acompañado, mon amour, tú estás siempre en mis pensamientos ¿Cómo hacértelo entender? Nuestro amor es la única base.

1/30/91

Te invito a la reflexión. Pensemos sobre nuestras dudas y preguntas. No pretendamos resolverlas. Es casi imposible. Solo tengámoslas presentes. Reconozcamos que lo que nos viene no es un jardín de rosas. (Hay alguien que acaso tenga un matrimonio o vida en común ideal?) Reconocer nuestros problemas es el primer paso para solucionarlos. Este

> proyecto de vida en común tiene sus bemoles. Es básico que estemos conscientes de ello, para que no nos agarre fuera de base. ¿Tú me entiendes? Lo único que tengo claro es mi amor por ti, ante cualquier circunstancia, mon amour. Je t'aime. C'est la verité!

*

FINALLY, RAMÓN AND I were alone. He visited my parents on weekends and vacationed with my mother. But he would never live with my parents again. It was my turn. At 25, I was fully responsible for my four-year-old son, providing for him the best way I could.

The truth was that I didn't know how to take care of a child. Where my mother had been cruel to me, with my son she was sweet. Did she act like that to turn the child against me, or was she paying her emotional debt by giving him what she didn't give me? Whatever the answer, I could not imitate her.

"We need to hurry up, Ramón. I need to be at school early today," I said while putting a box of cereal on the table with the milk, sugar, and a glass of orange juice.

While I made myself a cup of coffee, he fidgeted in his chair. I brought the coffee to the table expecting him to be half way through with the cereal. It was untouched.

"What's up? Why are you not eating the cereal?" I asked.

"There is a mosquito in my cereal," he said.

I took a close look at the bowl. "Nope. No mosquito," I said.

"There is a mosquito, but it's a tiny one. You can't see it."

"Here we go again," I protested.

"Can I have eggs?" he asked, looking at me with puppy eyes and a tender smile.

"OK. Eggs. How do you like them, hard or runny?"

"Not runny."

After a while, I emerged from the kitchen with one fried egg, over hard, and toast.

"Here you go. You want butter and jam on your toast?"

"Yes, please," he said. "But the egg is runny."

"It isn't. You know what? Just eat the toast, drink the juice, and let's get out of here. Can you do that for me?" I said in a voice that grew in its loudness. I could feel the steam blowing from my mouth.

That was a good day. The only way I had learned to deal with a child was through hitting and insulting, but I had made the conscious decision not to do that. Breaking from an abuse legacy is not as easy as saying, "I won't do that." I had to prepare myself for the great challenge.

*

IN JULY, I posted an ad in a newspaper to sublet a room to students. A professor from Universidad Simón Bolivar called saying he had a list of international students waiting for placement. Thus, I rented the spare room in Jussef's apartment to a series of foreign students that looked like hippies but provided a reliable income, while I struggled to pay my bills. They travelled inside the country to places I could only dream of: La Gran Sabana, Los Roques, Los Llanos.

Except for mattresses and a few kitchen utensils, the apartment was basic and bare. The only luxuries I could afford were the spectacular view of El Avila and the building's structure – a piece of architectural oddity, a perfect cylinder like a shampoo bottle in the middle of the busy Avenida Andrés Bello. I had only one rule: no drugs in the apartment.

I still owned the place in Guatire – the tiny apartment I bought with the Heinz severance package and rented out to pay the mortgage and to avoid selling property that could be useful later on. However, the mortgage rates suddenly spiked to 35%. Because my parents were co-signers of my mortgage, I didn't qualify for a government subsidy and was forced to sell at a loss.

*

JUSSEF SENT TICKETS to visit him in Cincinnati. Again, I left Ramón with my parents for two weeks for the Christmas break in 1989. Before returning to Venezuela, I stopped in New York to meet Zoë. It was the first break I had in years, and my friends gave me winter clothes to wear on the trip.

I waited for Zoë in her apartment on 98th and Broadway and glimpsed the life she wrote about—the life she wanted me to build for myself. A group of five adult women shared the rent and the chores. Of all the other women, Lisa was the closest friend. She looked very much like Zoë. They were both white, in their mid forties, with dark, short hair, long nose and radiant smiles. Lisa stirred something in a big pot in the kitchen, and two other women shared a beer in front of the TV, their feet up on the coffee table. When Lisa was done, she served each one of us a cup of the treat she was making.

"Arroz con leche! What's the word for this in English?" I asked.

"Rice pudding," said Lisa.

A red-haired woman filled the room with sounds from her saxophone, and we hushed to listen as we savored the dessert. They were best friends, all professional women making their own path in the world.

Zoë arrived later because she was still working when I first arrived. While she wriggled out of her gray business suit and silk blouse, she opened her neat bedroom to me. The bed took most of the space. It was one of those beds with shelves as a headboard - ample, functional, and comfortable. Her personal objects were carefully arranged in the shelves: books, her perfume, Anaïs Anaïs, and lipsticks.

"You can spend the night here. I have a date. I'll pick you up in the morning for breakfast," she said. She had changed into black slacks, comfortable shoes, and a delicate blouse in soft colors. That night, the sound of sirens and traffic never slowed. The hours melted into each other until daylight filtered through the window.

In the morning, she returned as promised. We strolled down Broadway and stopped at a diner for breakfast. Finally together, we picked up from our last letter.

"What do you think of my roommates?" Zoe asked.

"I like them. I liked Lisa and her rice pudding. They all seem easy going. It feels like you live with your grown-up sisters," I said.

"I'm so glad you say that. You seemed very comfortable with everyone. Usually people from here who find out the way I live are shocked. It's not very conventional to live in a group."

"Better than living with your parents until you are a grown up woman with a kid," I said.

Zoë smiled at me. "I'm sorry you didn't get to see my plays at the theater. The theater is such a big part of my life. We have a new show almost ready for revisions, 'Bushwhacked.' I'm so sorry you won't be here to see it. Anyway, tell me, how is Ramón? I got him a Bat Mobile."

She took little cars out of her purse arranging them on the table. A tiny Bat Mobile stood out. "We all need a Bat Mobile," she said.

"Ramón will love this. Thank you so much. You didn't have to worry," I said. "He's fine. We are finally getting settled together. It's really difficult. I don't know how to be a mom, and he is kind of bratty. If I may say so.".

"He has been spoiled. Your job is to learn how to guide his good behavior, bring out the best in him. By what you tell me in your letters, he is smart too. You also have to make sure to take time off from your many responsibilities. You need a break." She spoke fast as if she needed to hurry through every word. I had been used to reading her words, not listening to her fast speech pattern.

"I think he is learning English. He listens to me speaking to the international students I share the apartment with. The other day he came into the kitchen, looked at me, and started speaking gibberish. I guess he was trying to speak English. He can be very funny." I reached for her hand across the table. "Thanks again for all you do for me. I will never be able to repay you for all the support you have given me since we met."

"Don't say that. We're friends," she said, smiling at me tenderly.

"I wish I could stay here and not go back to my difficult life, but it's time to catch that plane back home. Can you visit me in Venezuela?"

"Not anytime soon. I will go on vacation around Easter time. I need a break. But we have to keep in touch. We have to keep writing and sending letters."

Zoë paid the bill. We put all the little cars in a bag and headed out of the diner onto Broadway.

Outside, we signaled for a cab. When it reached the curb, we held each other in a tight hug. I smelled her perfume and kept the memory of it for years to come, like a soft breeze easing away my dark cloud.

*

RAMÓN TUGGED AT my shirt and whispered, "I need to go to the bathroom."

"Go. I am busy."

We were in the Modern Language School of Universidad Central de Venezuela, an out of campus facility, on top of a steep hill in San Bernardino, a residential area in Caracas. I was taking a midterm for my Castellano class.

Two minutes later, Ramón came back into the classroom. "The bathroom is broken," he said in a whisper.

"Excuse me." I raised my hand. "Could I take a break to take my son to the bathroom?"

The teacher nodded her head in approval.

I was trying college once again. During the day, I took Ramón to a preschool nearby. On the days his school was out, I took him with me to classes. It was a verbal agreement with my professors, and for the most part, it didn't have any negative consequences.

We walked to a gathering of trees, and I told him to release himself there. He shook his head. We walked into the neighborhood and knocked on people's doors, and I asked if my son could use their bathroom. House after house slammed doors, and the boy still would not relieve himself behind a tree. Finally, one compassionate soul, an older woman, opened the door and let him use the bathroom. Back at the school building, the professor graciously allowed me back in to finish the test, but I flunked it. For another professor under similar circumstances, when my son developed a rash in the middle of my test, not only did she not allow me to take a break during the test, but she also let me know that I wasn't cut out for college.

"Try a secretarial job," she told me just outside her office the next day. "You know enough German to pass as a bilingual secretary. It's time to drop out."

*

MY FRUSTRATION CHANGED my posture and facial expression to reveal an angry woman. I hunched, frowned, and pursed my lips together. I insulted myself whenever I felt disappointed or contradicted. Crying spells preceded throwing objects within close proximity. There were always plenty of reasons to explode because the whole world seemed to conspire against me. A clerk tried to overcharge for a pound of cheese. Somebody was trying to get into the building without a key. The clientele of the sex workers on my street posed a threat to our safety. A bus driver wouldn't give me the student discount or give preferential fare to Ramón.

One bus driver asked Ramón, "How old are you?" Children under five didn't pay bus fare.

Ramón was proud to have grown so much and exclaimed, "I'm almost six!"

The driver spat out, "These women don't find a man to raise their kids and then want the free ride."

I stepped off the bus holding my son's hand, grabbed a rock lying on the sidewalk and threw it at the bus. The rock narrowly missed a window as the bus maneuvered away. Nothing happened, but it was a warning for me that I needed to pull myself together.

I had started college at 16 and dreamed of earning a doctorate. I would become an independent woman and a college professor or a translator. A few years later, I had completed only three semesters in college, had a five-year-old son, and lived for free in my boyfriend's apartment—a boyfriend who wasn't available or ready to make a commitment with us. I dropped out of college feeling like a pile of shards.

I took my anger around my child. I didn't hit him. I pounded doors, hit walls, and punched myself on the head or on my legs, instead of hurting him. He cried a lot and bit his nails. We continued our power struggles at meal times; he refused to eat, and I insisted on feeding him. I was so ill prepared.

Sitting on my living room floor, I looked at the magnificent view of El Avila. The mountain completely filled the view from any point of the small apartment located on the north side of the round building. A flock of blue, green and yellow Guacamayas flew past our balcony almost every morning when the humidity rose from the ground like inverted pouring rain. *It'd be so easy to fly away with the macaws.* Then, the Guacharacas croaked scandalously. I imagined my son living among them, feeding on cockroaches. No. If I took my life, then Ramón would be in my parents' care. *Not with them. Not ever. I imagined both of us flying with the Guacamayas, becoming colorful birds on the north side of the city, nesting in the mountains that separate the city from the sea, feeding on fruits, living a magnificent life.*

"I should take my mother's shit again," I wrote to Zoë. "Be what she wants me to be, comply, conform, and have it easy." Zoë would not hear of it. She wrote me a three-page single-spaced letter on repudiation.

> 6/1990
>
> You finally got your act together and moved out of your mother's house. Living with her was driving you crazy. You were constantly under her thumb, and under her scrutiny. She was always intimidating you, dictating how you should live and how you should raise your child. Am I right or wrong? And to be honest, my impression was that you were frightened of her – frightened to do what you wanted if it differed from what you thought she wanted you to do. So now you've finally moved out and into a potentially better living situation. You are free-er now

> to live the way you want; do what you want and date whom you want. BUT, it sounds to me like you are not taking advantage of this. Instead of using it to your advantage, it seems like you are "repudiating" – making your move forward feel like a move backward.

Her advice: I needed to save money, create a network of trustworthy friends around me, and use my language skills to find a good job. She saw that I was working tirelessly, but she wasn't sure where I was leading myself. "You need direction," she wrote.

Suicide contemplation became my daily battle, but my duty to Ramón kept me alive. Instead of harming him, I looked for help in whatever way I could to make sure that I never hurt my child in any way. I had a choice, and I made the right one.

*

ZOË SUGGESTED TO FOCUS on learning computer languages because it paid a lot of money. She reassured me she would always help, but that I needed to set goals for myself and work towards them.

> I don't really know what you want from your life – I only know that you can get it, and that you are getting it now. I'd be glad to help you in whatever ways I can, but you have to really want to make things better and be happier. Set some realistic goals for yourself. First and foremost is making friends. And then take it one step at a time from there. It's scary to go after what you want, but it's really important. If you don't do it, you will always be bitter and mad.

She finished her long letters with phrases my mother never said to me.

> You have so much going for you: you are pretty; you are bright and witty, and you're often very brave. You could be doing more with your life… and you could be much, much happier. Go for it!
>
> Love, Zoë

*

"AUNT EUNICE, my mom doesn't want to get up from bed." From my bed, I heard Ramón speaking on the phone in the narrow corridor of the round apartment.

Eunice demanded all children to call her aunt and called herself sister to all her friends. Thus, she became my sister and Ramón's auntie. She lived on the ground floor apartment in our building with her husband, Edgar. We met when Ramón fell down the parking lot stairs while showing me a bike trick he'd just learned. From the balcony of their apartment, they saw what happened, how I froze with fear while Ramón bled. Edgar ran downstairs and whisked the child in his arms. He ran to the clinic next door. Ramón fractured his pinky finger, and I met two wonderful people who would become my best friends in Venezuela. Eunice was only a couple of years older than I, and Edgar was sixteen years her senior.

"You have to get up to go to work," Eunice commanded. I heard her voice far and muffled as if Charlie Brown's teacher were asking me to go to school. My body had become an anvil, and I didn't have the strength to lift it.

"Pa' qué? Yo no quiero vivir más."

"Qué depre tan arrecha m'hija! Fucking blues! But right now you have to get up to go to work. If not, you'll get fired. You need the money to support your son. Párate m'hija! Get up." Eunice pulled both my legs out of the bed and placed them on the floor. She grabbed my arms and commanded me with a firm voice to pull myself together and get in the shower. She opened the cold-water faucet and pushed me in. "Get up. I know it's hard. I have been there, but you have a child. You don't have permission to get sick or die."

I made it to work that day. In the evening, Eunice told me that she had made me an appointment with a psychologist. "Her name is Irene Gutierrez. You'll like her."

At the therapist's office, the psychologist introduced herself and offered a chair for me to sit in.

"My name is Irene Gutierrez. Eunice spoke highly of you." I raised my eyes to finally see her, a white woman with long hair falling on her back. She sat across from me in an armchair. A miniature Buddha figure and a brass bowl adorned her side table. I started speaking but couldn't express more than one thought before breaking down in tears.

Irene observed and took notes. "You are clearly depressed, and it's severe. You'll need to take medication," she said after watching me sob for about ten minutes.

Irene referred me to a psychiatrist for medication. The psychiatrist recommended Prozac, which I took for a few weeks until I started feeling better. Then I stopped. I couldn't afford medication, and I didn't have insurance. Instead, I promised myself to make the most of the monthly appointments with Irene. In her tiny office, she helped me find ways of coping with the suicidal ideation.

Back at Irene's office, I continued relating my misfortunes and frustrations between sobs.

"The first thing we are going to do is try to organize your life. At the moment, it looks overwhelming," she said as she handed me another tissue. "You are a single mother, trying to finish college and work at the same time.

You don't have enough money to pay the bills. Your boyfriend is in the United States, and you are estranged from your family. We can't take care of everything at the same time. Let's start with the most urgent, the relationship with your son."

With Irene's guidance, Ramón and I settled into a livable situation. I designed a chart to track the conflicts with Ramón on a calendar so that I could identify the problem areas and our strengths. Every day, I decorated the chart with clouds, suns, or lightning bolt cutouts I had made to let Ramón see his behavior for the day. Little by little, I worked my way up to accepting the illustrated weather of my life.

I helped Ramón make good choices, like picking up his toys or clothes from the ground, doing homework on time, and not fussing at meals. I learned to avoid power struggles and to pick my battles more effectively. Eventually, he slept alone in his bed and ate whatever mamá put on the table. I give him all the credit for this. I was actually a terrible cook. Sometimes my meals looked like barf. I deposited gobs of a sort of green gravy in a soup dish and placed it front of him.

"What's that?" he asked.

"Spinach cream soup," I said.

Edgar and Eunice, and then Patricia, another great friend, taught me a few easy recipes of pasta sauces and nutritious soups. I grew more considerate of my skinny, lactose intolerant picky eater.

Organization allowed me to really get to know my son. Ramón was exceptionally smart, lively, cheerful, and a pleasure to be with. He was active and interested in many activities. After a weekend of careful thinking, he chose to take on violin instead of karate. I could only afford one or the other. I worked overtime for several months to afford a violin that needed repairs too frequently. Ramón bumped the case on bus doors, under his bed, and in the elevator. We always had to scout for cheap luthier services. It was well worth it to see him joyfully sitting on the toilet to play his violin. "It sounds great in here, mamá."

The stressful weekdays gave way to slow Sundays. We rode our bikes along El Parque Los Caobos and would stop to eat raspados. Surrounded by tall mahoganies at La Plaza Los Museos, we licked the shaved ice to cool down from the tropical heat. Skin and bone both of us, we looked like siblings growing up together despite the 21-year gap between us. We sat on park benches to listen to storytellers as they filled our imagination with fantastic characters and impossible fables. Other Sundays, we would ride our bicycles to the Aula Magna of Universidad Central de Venezuela, the concert hall of the university I no longer attended, to listen to free concerts by the Municipal Orchestra.

"Mamá, apúrate!" he shouted while running uphill on the trails of El Avila National Park. "Mira mamá," he said pointing his index finger as if he had just discovered the city at the foot of the mountain. Our hands dirty, we sat on the side of the trail to eat our lunches: sandwiches, bananas, and boxed juice. When we finished, we continued uphill, through the magnificent park. He would stop now and then to show me bugs or rocks, the things that most attracted him. Sometimes I became distracted by the incredible amount of different species of flowers and plants, or by listening to the call of the cristofué, the large flycatcher nesting inside the forest. On those occasions, I had to run to catch up with him afraid of losing my skinny boy. By the end of the day, when both of us were too exhausted to even talk, we walked back to the city to a cold shower and a spaghetti dinner. Ramón loved the adventure and I enjoyed watching him grow confident, his bright eyes looking up at me. On those days, we were fulfilled, happy to be alive.

The Study of Scars

I CONSULTED A DOCTOR about a respiratory problem, and with one look at my face, he was intrigued. He touched the blackheads on my chin and around my nose ever so slightly with the tip of his fingers. Then grabbed a magnifying glass and explored my neck and down my back. Silently.

I wasn't new to this exploration of my skin. I had tried all through my teenage years to stop the profusion of zits and blackheads on my face. The pores were deep and got dirty, causing frequent infections. I often consulted doctors about it, but it was the first time an ear, nose and throat doctor had noticed. As he magnified my skin, his silence made me think what he saw was really bad.

The day of my follow-up appointment, there was another doctor, old and wrinkled, a relic of a man.

"Lisbeth, I want you to meet Dr. Máximo. He headed the dermatology department of the Hospital Universitario for 40 years and is now retired."

Dr. Máximo brought some observation instruments and looked carefully at my skin. "Never seen this before," he said.

He made an appointment with me to meet on the eighth floor of the Hospital Universitario. When I arrived, several physicians and an aura of venerability surrounded the ancient doctor.

"I am already retired." His eyes looked serene, calm. "I will leave you with this team of leading research dermatologists to determine the nature of your peculiar condition."

Now I was intrigued. I wanted to know what it was. At Hospital Universitario, a team of professionals asked me to take my clothes off in front of them all: students, interns, teaching doctors, and research doctors. I had seen some of them before in their private practices when they were unable to cure me of whatever was happening to my face. I was now a specimen, the object of their attention, and felt uncomfortable.

"Does anybody else in your family have this?" one asked. They all looked the same to me, with their white coats, looking into my face as if in a close up.

"My brother has it, and so does my mother, several of her cousins, one of her uncles, and one of her brothers. My holes and pimples are a lot smaller than theirs. My mother and I look a lot like each other, specially here in the chin." I wasn't shy about volunteering information.

"Does it hurt?" a young intern asked.

"No."

"Have you been treated before?" a female student about my age spoke, while several of the doctors suddenly looked at their shoes. The light came through large floor to ceiling windows overlooking the university campus. To my right, there were a regular doctor's office bed and white shelves with medicine and equipment to the right of the room. The group of doctors stood in the middle facing me. Covered with a flimsy hospital gown, I felt exposed.

"I've seen about every dermatologist in Caracas. They've done cleansings. They used chemical peelings, gave me Vitamin A-Acid and Retinol." I continued answering their questions.

A short man with an arrogant air in his manner leaned in. "You know you can go to the beach only at nights, don't you?" he asked. He had a camera and snapped intrusive pictures of my face.

"No, I didn't know that. Nobody has mentioned sun before," I said. The students continued taking notes and murmuring among themselves.

I greeted an elegant female doctor I had met before. The arrogant doctor asked her, "Have you treated the patient before?"

"Yes. It didn't work."

"It doesn't surprise me, Doctor, that you were unable to treat her," he spat. Click, click went the camera.

"Do you have this anywhere else on your body, or is it just the face?" a different woman doctor asked.

"I'm kind of embarrassed: in the labia." I pointed at my genitals. "Also in the folding of the joints, chest, back, behind my legs, armpits. I also get zits on my scalp from time to time. They are gross," I said while the camera clicked around my neck.

"What do you think?" they asked each other.

"Comedones," said one, while others shrugged.

They left me alone and went to consult with each other.

Dr. Lucio, the short arrogant dermatologist who seemed to be the leader, delivered their conclusion when they came back. "We don't know what you have, but we want to know and we want to cure you. We are going to take some tissue from the face and the chest and send it to a pathologist to try to figure out what it is. The only thing for sure is that it's not common, and none of us knows how to treat it." He then directed a nurse to prepare me for a biopsy.

Another doctor hovered over my shoulder. "We also want to see as many of your relatives as we can. Do you think you can send some of them our way?" Dr. Lucio continued.

"I can ask my mother, and also my cousin. Other than that I don't know who else might be available for this. They don't seem to care as much as I do."

"Whoever comes in is fine. Tell them we are conducting research about this rare skin condition and would like to examine them to determine who has it and who doesn't," continued Doctor Lucio.

While the rest of the group dissolved, a specialty student, a fully built woman with an Italian last name did the intake interview.

"Do you suffer from any other conditions?"

"I have stomach problems. I throw up a lot and have frequent heartburn," I said.

"Psychiatric problems, depression, schizophrenia?"

"I suffer from depression."

"What do you take for that? Do you see a doctor regularly?"

"Nope. I cry a lot and seem to be miserable most of the time, but I have had a hard life. A doctor gave me Prozac. I only took it for a short while."

"Why?" she pressed on.

"It's expensive. I can barely pay my bills. I am a single mother."

"How are you feeling today?"

"I am fine. I am fine most of the time. It's just that from time to time I get really sad and want to die."

She wrote "manic-depressive" on the intake form.

Weeks later, when the results of the biopsy were back, they asked me to attend a conference. Dermatologists from across the nation came to the gathering. They presented my case with a slide projector in a large auditorium. Most of the information I knew, but now they were naming my condition for the first time a the group of physicians.

I felt like the Elephant Man.

"Dowling Degos Disease," Dr. Lucio announced from the podium. "It's a rare skin condition without a known cure. More frequent manifestations of this condition are present in the armpits and the groin. To the common eye, DDD looks like a three day old beard and unshaved armpits." He said this while pointing at pictures of my face, with the eyes covered with a black stripe, reflected on a large screen in the front of the room.

"Occasionally, DDD also shows on the face and vulva." I knew he was right.

"On the face, the hyper-pigmented web pattern becomes a profusion of black heads around the mouth, nose and chin, along with depressed acne scars - minus the acne." On and on the lecture continued.

At the end of the presentation, the group of doctors came to see me. One by one, they looked closely at my face. Some took pictures. Others asked more questions.

"I like your subject," one doctor said. "She has one kid," another one mentioned, while I said in a whisper, "I am not an elephant, I am a human being." Nobody seemed to notice.

Dr. Lucio and his assistant scheduled me for a dermabrasion. I didn't have to pay for the surgery, but they asked for helium, and I had to pay for that. I had to import the helium from another country just for the procedure.

"Can you do me a favor?" I asked Zoë on the phone.

"Yes, tell me what you need," she said.

After I explained to her about the doctors' research on my face and that they were asking me for helium, she said, "Lisbeth, there is nothing wrong with your face. I don't know why you need surgery in the first place, but I'll send you whatever you need. Wait for the package in the mail."

On the day of the surgery, I stepped out of the elevator on the eighth floor of the Hospital Universitario with the box of eight bottles of helium that Zoë had sent.

A nurse called my name from the door of the outpatient procedures room. I handed her the helium. She asked me to strip off my clothes and put on the hospital gown. I lay on the bed waiting for the doctor, and calming my nerves by observing the bright light coming through the window. When the doctor and his assistant finally came in, he turned the powerful surgery light on my face. This blinded me, and although I was awake the whole time, I couldn't see their faces.

Dr. Lucio explained what they were about to do. They would freeze the skin of my face with helium and then use a rotary tool to peel the epidermis off my chin. I was tense and gripped the rail of the bed.

I felt the anesthesia going in first, and then helium spray, and my skin going numb and hard like a piece of wood. Then I heard the rotary tool nearing my face. It sounded like a dentist drill. The perforating sound penetrated my ears and fear and hesitation shot through my body. Later, I felt a scrape across my chin and the upper left side of my face, near the temple. They came down again to the chin, found a small tumor, and decided to remove it. It was deep, and deeper they went with the rotary tool. I growled. Like at the dentist's office, I knew it would hurt later.

The tumor was on the left side of my chin. I could hear them talking in medical jargon, explaining what they saw: follicular plugs, retention cysts, trichoepithelioma, melanocytes, and hyper-pigmented epidermal projections in a filliform pattern, reticulated. In five excruciatingly long minutes, it was over.

The nurse used plenty of gauze to soak up some thick liquid coming out of the place they had worked on. I didn't see anything. The nurse said, "After 24 hours, remove the bandages. With the tip of your fingers, peel off the white film that will start growing on the wound. Don't let a scab grow, or it will cause a scar." She then explained in meticulous detail how to clean the wound and how to replace the bandages.

As directed, twenty-four hours later at home, I took off the bandages in front of the bathroom mirror. I let out a scream of horror. The lower part of my face was monstrously swollen. The skin below the lower lip was raw meat, the bare dermis out, bleeding a gooey gelatin mess. On the left side of the chin, there was what looked like a hole in the flesh. It was painful to see, and I started crying.

Diligently, I set out to do everything I was told, but I could not remove the white film, as I had been instructed. The wound was deeper than the dermis, and untouchable without anesthesia. I tried again and screamed. It was impossible. I wondered what on earth they had done.

I went to the doctor the next day, and they gave me medication for the pain. Every day, I cleaned the rest of the wound until the new skin began to grow, still red as raw meat. I didn't touch the little corner on the left; I abandoned it to its pain and its infection. Soon a scab began to grow. Later a thick keloid formed on the little round spot on the left of my chin.

The new skin came out lighter than my usual tone. The keloid was treated with steroids, which caused more pain, but at least the infection was gone. After a couple of months, I was able to resume my life without bandages. Darkening of the skin followed, with dark spots covering the dermabration area, as is common among non-white patients. With it came the slow and painful acceptance of my scar as part of my identity.

As soon as I healed from the wound and I didn't feel pain on my face, I continued to obsess over the blackheads on my face, constantly picking them or squeezing out their filth between my fingers. After I finished abusing my cheeks or forehead, I scrubbed with sugar or a soft brush, leaving my skin red and shiny, like cellophane paper, and disinfected with rubbing alcohol. The dermabration didn't cure Dowling Degos and scarred me for life.

When I still believed in prayer, I prayed to be beautiful, to have perfect skin, or at least for a miracle to remove the blemishes and the scar. But I stopped believing long ago.

Fortunately, skin is the only organ in the body that heals itself. It slowly grows back and resumes its function of protecting the body from the environment. As an undesired effect of the dermabration, sun exposure is detrimental to my skin. Hyperpigmentation has caused more blemishes, and blackheads are abundant on my face. But it doesn't hurt anymore.

I wear sunscreen by the pound and have a hat ready to go whenever I set out to hike or powerwalk. If I need to, I wear enough make up to cover the dark spots, but for the most part I put up with people looking at my face for too long, and with little kids asking stupid questions, like "Are you a mom or a dad?" From time to time, when I feel frustrated with people staring at my face, or people asking me if I am angry, I go to the bathroom and scream at my image in the mirror.

"Fea, eres fea," I cry.

Once a Great Nation

BY THE TIME Jussef came back from Cincinnati, I worked full time as a German-Spanish bilingual secretary in a bilateral project between the Venezuelan and German governments. I also translated occasionally for a private client. And I had been sharing Jussef's apartment with Mary, a girl from the Andes, who would soon move to Canada. We split cleaning chores and expenses equally. I felt she was my friend more than my tenant.

When I had visited Jussef a year earlier, we talked about getting married. Now, wedding plans got pushed to the bottom of the list as he unpacked his cardboard boxes and his gringo graduate degree. Readjusting took effort; so many loose ends threatened our noticeably shakier relationship. Ramón, now seven-years-old, played with the unopened boxes in the round apartment on Avenida Andrés Bello. I pushed the boxes around to sweep and mop the floor of the tiny apartment. We were living in a never-ending transition. Wedding talk changed to discussing the possibility of continuing the relationship while living separate lives. We never made a decision either way.

After considering my options, I quit my job, asked for a student loan, and went back to college to complete my BA in Modern Languages. I transferred to Universidad Metropolitana, a small private school with a semester system that allowed me to work part time as a freelance translator. If things didn't work out with Jussef and me, I wanted to have a complete education.

*

RAMÓN'S TEACHER KEPT sending notes home saying the child had misplaced his homework because he didn't write his name on the papers.

"What's wrong? This is the tenth time the teacher sends the same note. Why can't you write your name?" I asked one day, frustrated at dealing with the same annoying problem again.

"I don't want that name," he answered.

"Why?"

"I can write Ramón Perez or Clint Eastwood, but I don't want to write my name. I want to have Jussef's name," he said from behind his glasses.

I was flabbergasted. My seven-year-old son was having an identity crisis. How was I supposed to solve this problem?

"I'll adopt him," Jussef said.

Although passionate, ours wasn't an easy relationship, and we didn't think how it might affect the child if we decided to split. The adoption was just an idea that lingered for a while, retreated, and then showed up again every so often.

*

THE SUN SHINED strong through the north facing windows of the round apartment on Avenida Andrés Bello. We had upgraded from a mattress on the floor to a queen sized bed placed at the perfect angle to have a mountain view while lying down. But sleeping in on the weekends proved to be difficult with a regular phone call early on Saturday mornings, which invariably became an opportunity for screaming arguments.

"The phone is ringing," I said.

"Well, why don't you pick up?" Jussef asked.

"Because it's your mother. The phone is still ringing." I replied. "Aló."

The silence at the other end of the line felt like a bucket of icy water on my face.

"It's your mother, and she hung up," I said as the phone rang again. "There she is again. Take the damned call! She won't talk to me."

"Hola, mamá! ¿Cómo estás? Yes, we can go for lunch tomorrow." A soft lisp stressed each "s."

Jussef's mother was the main cause of our fights.

I crossed my arms over my chest. "Why did you say we will go for lunch tomorrow? I am not going." I turned to him with pursed lips and a frown.

"Yes, you are," he commanded.

"Jussef. What happened to our cultural Sundays, when we went to the Aula Magna to listen to concerts? Now we have to show up at your mother's house every Sunday and she is not nice. I don't care if she is not nice to me, but she is not nice to Ramón. Actually, she is mean."

"I can't change my mother." I watched his sad eyes framed by his thick eyebrows, his aquiline nose extending long and sensual. "We have to be stronger than anything else if we want our relationship to work out. You have to understand that her moral system belongs to another century." Irritated, his nostrils widened, and his eyebrows met at the center.

I looked at his face, reading it for signs of hatred, something to tell me that indeed it was over, that it was a mistake for us to continue. Instead, I saw his lips moving. I saw his sad eyes looking at me from the memories of movies we watched together, our nights looking at stars, and our shared orgasms.

"Great. Then explain it to me," I said, "Why am I the one who always has to make the effort to understand others? Why can't anybody make an effort to understand me? Why don't you ask her to understand me, to leave us alone? ¿Por qué no pones los puntos sobres las íes? I have to be forgiving, understanding, holier than thou. ¡Coño e' la madre! I am not a nun or a Buddhist monk. I have feelings and they get hurt every fucking week."

"My family is very important in my life. You have to accept that." His nostrils showed how much effort he had put into the sentence. "I can't leave my mother on her own." Jussef always said that. We had to carry on with a pebble in the shoe that felt like a boulder.

In therapy a few weeks later, I discussed my relationship with Irene. From her armchair in her small office, she helped analyze my situation. She said she didn't see a way out, but that we always surprised her, the way we stood together again in the most difficult moments. "Lisbeth, he has his own baggage – a mother who won't see you in good light because you don't meet any of her expectations for her son. She is going to try every trick in the book to break you guys apart. You decide if you are going to put up with it or call it quits."

I wanted to run from her office. I didn't want a rational explanation of why people behave the way they do. Why couldn't I be loved like everyone else? Wasn't it enough to have the mother I had? Now life threw in a future mother-in-law-from-hell as well?

She leaned forward in her chair and pressed her palms together. "Even more, he feels he is giving a lot by taking you with a kid when he had other options, probably other wealthy Arab women handpicked by his family, or modern women he met in the U.S. Who knows?" She leaned back in her chair. "Maybe he needs to play around a bit more before committing to you."

It was a lot to take in. I started to cry, but Irene pressed on. "On the other hand, you have your baggage. You are not an easy person."

"Wait a minute," I protested.

"Listen, Lisbeth. You get depressed often, and it can get ugly with your thoughts of suicide and all. You are seriously traumatized. You have anger issues and a tendency to become violent, but you are learning to live. You are so smart and lost that you are a danger to yourself."

I couldn't hear anymore and broke down crying. She continued in a quiet voice. "The person who loves you must be a special kind of person. I think he is special, and he can give you the kind of calm love you need, but he needs more time. I don't see how it can work right now."

But we didn't break up. Instead, Jussef initiated procedures to adopt Ramón.

*

ON FEBRUARY 2, 1992, the phone rang early in the dark of the morning. I rolled on my side of the bed, pulled the sheet over my shoulders and found comfort in my pillow, refusing to answer. "It must be your mother," I said as Jussef reached for the phone.

"Golpe de Estado? Coup d'état? Are you sure?" Jussef asked while I glanced at the window noticing the day breaking the dark night.

"Who is it?" I asked.

"My sister," Jussef said while muting the receiver with his hand.

We heard small airplanes flying low on the city, and explosions in the distance. Jussef, Ramón and I browsed the TV and radio for news. Nothing. We went to get the newspaper at the corner kiosk and chatted with neighbors, who were equally intrigued. Finally, at around noon, the president appeared on TV, assuring the country that nothing was happening, and that the situation was under control. Yet machine gun shots could be heard in the background. We learned later that the president had broadcast from a bunker.

In the early afternoon, we took the elevator to the rooftop, and from our privileged position at the Torre Andrés Bello, we witnessed bits of the air fight that was taking place over Aeropuerto La Carlota – a small military landing strip on the east side of Caracas. The smell of burnt jet fuel reached us. The airplanes flew close to El Avila, then made a u-turn above La Cota Mil and headed southeast where the airplanes disappeared from view. Clouds of smoke rose from the La Carlota area.

Most people remained in their houses. Edgar came to the rooftop to tell us to go back to our place. "You could get shot," he yelled at us. The news broadcasted images of small tanks at the Palacio de Miraflores gate, the presidential house, where rebels and the loyal army engaged in battle. By that night, we knew it wasn't a joke. The president had lied when he said that nothing was happening. Somebody had tried to kill him, an elected president.

Ramón took his Fisher Price cassette recorder and microphone and pretended to interview people about the current events going on. "¿Cuál es su opinión?" he asked to his amused and worried parents and neighbors.

A young lieutenant colonel named Hugo Chavez, handcuffed and surrounded by armed soldiers loyal to the president, spoke that afternoon to the Venezuelan people still stunned by the sudden turn of events. "I take full responsibility for the events of today, and for now, I ask my fellow comrades to put down their guns."

Eventually the Congress ousted the president on counts of embezzlement and corruption, but the young colonel remained in prison for attempted assassination. As a result of Chavez's adventures, we had to live through a period of martial law, which included a curfew after dark and a temporary loss of the right to assembly. Also, we understood we could be arrested and our houses searched without a warrant.

From our balcony, we watched the day close on the Barrio Los Manolos. After 4 p.m. women and men hurried home with concerned looks on their faces, clutching their belongings or children close to them. Once in the middle of the night, I heard "ALTO" in the back alley. I ran to the balcony to see a police car parked at the end of the street, a man hurriedly walking towards El

Barrio Los Manolos holding a bag or groceries. The policeman drew his gun and repeated, "ALTO." The man stopped, and two policemen searched him. Then they put a gun to the back of his head and motioned for him to get in the trunk of the cab. I couldn't hear his pleas, but we saw him climbing into the trunk. The policemen shut the trunk and sped away.

Not that Venezuela was rich in civil liberties to begin with, but the country's politicians kept their corrupt ways while Chavez evolved into a new warlord in jail.

The media flocked to Chavez's prison cell, fascinated with the bravery of the young military man with a penchant for impromptu, visceral speeches. From his new celebrity status, he spoke about corruption, about Venezuelan Air Force pilots flying politicians' mistresses on their private trips, and a never-ending tirade of complaints justifying his violent actions in early February. Arias Cárdenas, Chavez's closest associate, attempted a second coup in November of that same year. He didn't succeed either. We joked that if this was what Venezuela counted on to defend her from foreign invasion, we were doomed.

Between the political unrest and the economic situation, common crime was on the rise and populated the evening news. But the government was busy controlling its young soldiers and fighting impeachment in the congress. The social and political stability of the greatest economy in Latin American was lost one coup d'état and one-armed robbery at a time.

*

AT FIRST, ZOË didn't like Jussef. She thought he was arrogant and inconsiderate and started to send money for a new *start my own life fund.* Her letters would end with a note: "Call me to let me know if you see General Jackson at the bottom of this letter, and we'll do the same in the next one."

I read her letters carefully and put the twenty-dollar bill in a box labeled "My Going Away Fund," but continued with the adoption process. My ambivalence about Jussef, a shaded area between loving him dearly and despising the differences that separated us, caused me a great deal of anxiety. I couldn't let go of a man who gave me so much joy even though I felt he would never accept me if his family didn't approve. We lived two different lives: one of security and stability, and one of obstacles and dysfunctionality.

During the week, Jussef left at 5:30 a.m. for his job at the oil research institute out of town while I readied Ramón for school. We then rode a crowded bus to downtown on the beautiful Avenida Andrés Bello lined with Sandbox trees. Under the Fuerzas Armadas Bridge, Avenida Andrés Bello becomes Avenid Urdaneta, a busy urban corridor, humming with life from the earliest hours of the morning. From the bus windows, my son and I watched the mosaic sidewalks filled with people rushing to government jobs or opening the stores of the downtown wholesalers.

"How do you know where to get off the bus?" Ramón asked.

"Just look for El Avila. That's always in the north. Look for the churches. Those are your reference points." I never got lost in those streets.

We would stop at Santa Capilla and walk four blocks north to Colegio La Salle de Tienda Honda, an old Catholic School in the heart of the historic district, through narrow streets with three to five-story apartment buildings on each side. After I left my son at the large wooden doors of his school, I walked south to catch the subway east to the end of the line and catch another bus to Universidad Metropolitana. Fortunately, Caracas is in a small valley, and on the metro, you can cross it quickly

At noon, I took a ride downtown, picked up my son at school, and returned to the college with him to continue my afternoon classes. I asked the language school dean's permission to attend classes with my son. "I promise he won't bother anybody," I said at our initial meeting.

I always carried Lego blocks, books and his little violin with me. He knew everybody and volunteered to buy snacks for my classmates in the cafeteria in exchange for a candy bar. He learned English in my college classes. This time, I excelled at school, earning the respect of my classmates and the consideration of my teachers.

At 28, I was the oldest of my classmates, who were mostly older teenagers experimenting with sex and separating themselves from their parents. I was the grown-up, the single mother who had outread them all, wrote five papers every week, and engaged professors in academic discussions. I tutored my classmates in the cafeteria or my apartment and enjoyed their young, fresh company. They had no idea the kind of life I had lived.

The Modern Language program had three components: English as a Foreign Language, Culture, and Teaching. Students were required to write an undergraduate thesis: a book of no fewer than 200 pages. I chose to write about Sonia Sanchez, a southern black American poet, who, from a black feminist perspective, was the angriest of the civil rights movement poets.

I first came in contact with her work from loose photocopies of her book of poetry, *Homecoming*, not in the brick-size anthologies of American literature. I found her irreverent verses were meant to be spoken and not read. In the elective sociolinguistic (Language and Society) class, I learned that Sanchez's work was consistent with oral tradition, the origins of African American literature. In her voice, I recognized the discourse of a black woman with high social consciousness, reflected in the linguistic marks in her verses, symbols of her reality: spitting bullets, slow suicides in seclusion, black magic. When I reviewed critics of her work, I found that their insights were aggressive towards, even disdainful of the quality of her poetry. But what I saw as a reader who already had the grain of feminism growing in me was the role of the black woman as a talented artist, a committed teacher, and community mother. She was the role model I wanted to identify with.

The anger in Sanchez's work appealed to me because I identified with the black woman "with razor blades between her teeth." Sanchez was a poet/teacher and single mother who, between lectures and poetry readings, acted as umpire in the baseball games of her children. Black people all throughout The Americas shared the history of the pain of slavery. Although I only experienced colorism as a form of racial discrimination, I identified with the struggle of the African American women portrayed in Sanchez's poetry. I am a light skin negro woman, half of whose ancestors came to this side of the world in shackles, while the other half had whips in their hands.

*

JUSSEF AND I MADE plans and decisions as if we were a married couple. We purchased an office space for rental income and a second car so that I could finally learn to drive. He drove the new car and handed me down the blue Lada, a Russian-made compact car, with a clutch that would not cooperate while driving up Caracas' many hills. I burned from the inside out while driving from our apartment in La Florida to El Centro to Ramón's school to Universidad Metropolitana in the eastern outskirts of town. As I changed gears, I had to put the tip of my foot under the clutch to release it. Maddening.

At the Aula Magna, Universidad Central's performance center and the country's main political platform, students chanted, "Chavez, Chavez. Golpe, golge," a strong call for a coup d'état. I heard this and other worrying accounts of the growing support for Chavez in Sabana Grande, where coffee shop philosophers, intellectuals, and writers discussed politics, art, and cultural events, sitting comfortably in rattan chairs under a blue sky. I wasn't part of an intellectual circle but knew where to go for information and opinions.

The Congress elected an interim president before the expedited elections, but the political decline of what used to be a great nation was already underway. I thought the country was lost. Chavez had read two books in his life: the *Communist Manifesto* and Bolivar's Letters. An ignorant megalomaniac, he mixed the two books and came up with a new dogma. I had been a militant leftist in my teens. When I was 18, I voted in my first election at a school in my neighborhood. I saw three of my fellow comrades in line at the polling station. We made small talk, reassured ourselves of the growing movement, and acknowledged the slim chances of winning any posts. When the votes were counted, my political party got zero votes at that station. This meant at least my vote had been stolen.

Left or right, the country's authorities didn't know how to play clean. Every aspect of our society was smeared by "compadrazgo." Anyone reaching a position of authority immediately moved his friends and associates into the lower ranks of his organization, and those who were supposed to keep watch didn't care as long as they got a piece of the pie. Small government employees accepted bribes for ID cards and driver's licenses. The cheese vendor hacked the balance to give himself a bigger cut. The bus driver pocketed some of the day's earnings. Not capitalism or socialism, but corruption is the country's form of government. I never again voted in Venezuela.

Oil money continued to flow abundantly into Venezuela, but it never reached those who most needed it. Chavez wouldn't change that; his preoccupation was power. With his military background, I didn't see how the country would move to reinforce democracy. A visceral speaker, Chavez knew how to tap into the country's resentment after decades of corruption. Incendiary public speaking didn't make him a great leader, though. It made him a caudillo that would soon bring the country to its destruction.

*

BY THIS POINT, Jussef was paying for my son's education at a modest, private school and helping out with homework time. Signs of a structured family life began to show in our little household. He made a rule that we have kept to this day, of sitting at the table together for dinner with shirts and shoes on, no complaints.

"Dinner time is sacred," he said. Not even in the height of our fights, when I called Jussef names, cursed or threw a glass on the floor, did he flinch on this rule.

"Do you think you are superior because you don't get angry?" I screamed at him, strands of my hair between my fingers.

"One person losing control is enough," he replied with his nostrils suspended well above his moustache line.

That night we sat at dinner and ate arroz con pollo, my comfort food of choice, a one-pot dish that included all three main food groups in a delicious medley seasoned with curry.

Cockroach in the Armoire

MY MOTHER HAD a habit of showing up unannounced at our apartment door.

"Hola, mi amor querido. ¿No le das un beso a tu agüelita?" she said, sweet as a lime, her dentured smile too precise.

"¡Mamá!" I clasped my hands in an attempt to stay calm. "I have told you a thousand times, you have to call before showing up."

She looked matronly, not the hot mama she had been in her twenties and thirties, clad in polyester pants and a comfortable blouse without any grace. She scanned me from top to bottom and spat, "You have always been a whore. Now you think you are a lady, and I have to request a hearing to see you?" My son stood silently nearby, while my veins disintegrated from acid.

She chose to make these visits on weekdays to avoid Jussef because she had decided he was the reason I was so cold to her. On the occasions I hired help, somebody to watch my son for a few hours in the afternoon, my mother often befriended the sitter, so that she would be allowed in the apartment when I wasn't home. I would open the door and see her sitting on my couch, or scurrying from my bedroom like a cockroach suddenly caught in the open when the lights turn on, where she surely had been had skittering through my drawers.

My vibrator, which looked like a little electric massage ball, was tucked discreetly beneath my underwear in the bedroom closet. After one of those unannounced visits, I discovered its cable had been cut.

"Did you do this?" I asked Ramón.

"No, but Grandma was in your drawers," he said.

I asked the sitter why she had allowed my mother in. "Esa es su mamá. Ella tiene derecho."

"You know what? ¡Yo tengo derecho! I have the right to decide who comes into my house and who doesn't. I have the right to live without fear," I said. I opened the door for her to leave. She collected her purse, exited the apartment, and called the elevator. I rested my back on the closed front door.

"Back to square one. First thing: childcare," I said to myself.

*

I DIDN'T KNOW then that one could extract the "mean mother" from one's chest—the cockroach I held inside paralyzing me with fear. I would wake up sweating, screaming and kicking, shaking the monsters that threatened my body – mostly giant cockroaches. Jussef, always compassionate in those moments, held me tight and whispered reassuring words. He would turn on the lights and offer me a glass of water, caressing my hair until I fell back to sleep.

*

I GREW UP in Los Naranjos, a small village-like subdivision of government housing in the outskirts of Guarenas, probably 50 miles east of Caracas, where we identified our neighbors by their occupations: the policeman, the factory worker, the nurse, the teacher. In the common areas, the boys played baseball with the lids of beer bottles, using broomsticks for bats, while the girls jumped rope under the acacia trees. During the rainy season, when the sky closed with heavy rain, the children played in the torrential downpour and "swam" in the downhill "rivers" on our sidewalks.

If we lingered too long when it was time to go inside, my mother yelled the collective name of her brood, Los Coimans, and waited for us at the door of the flat roof duplex with a belt in her right hand and a bucket of salty water by her side. She dipped the leather belt in the salty water and struck our backs one by one. I was always the last in line, waiting with wide eyes for what would soon happen. Sometimes I peed my pants in anticipation.

My father, in those days, enjoyed the ambiguous flexibility of a long commute to and from work in the city while my mother stayed home with the kids. The unpredictability of his commute filled with all sorts of unexpected obstacles: accidents, mudslides, and increasing traffic as the small agricultural Guarenas grew into a suburb. Without telephones to find out her husband's whereabouts, my mother frequently worried about my father's constant delays in the city. My father used this freedom to his benefit.

By the time I was four years old, it was already evident to most adults around us that all the passion had been drained from my parents' union, and resentment had accumulated. As Catholics, they had married for the rest of eternity in a textbook example of dysfunction. On the days my father was "delayed," my mother told anyone who wanted to hear, "I have a pair of shears to cut his penis off one of these nights."

While my father was off to work and later doing who-knows-what, my mother served lunch and had an impeccable house before noon every day. After the lunch dishes were done and put away, she turned the TV on and sat down to do elaborate crochet projects. Her remarkable stamina and resourcefulness equaled only to her cruelty and coarseness in the way she channeled her increasing anger and dissatisfaction. On the refrigerator door, she posted lists of possible "crimes" and their respective penalty in strokes of the belt: a random sock on the floor, five strokes; undone bed, ten strokes; dirty underwear on the floor, fifteen strokes, and so on.

My siblings and I endured her beatings as much as her inexperienced cooking. Lunch began with a spoonful of codfish oil to help us grow strong. The meal was served in prison-like metal trays with compartments for different food types. Manners were not a concern. We could burp or fight each other at the table without risking punishment, but we had to eat without protesting, no matter how inedible the food looked. I was a picky eater. She pulled my hair down, and when my head tilted back and I screamed, "Agg," she forced the spoonful of soup down my throat. If I refused to eat, she stored the food and served it again for the next meal. If I vomited, I had to eat that, too.

When I was about five years old, my mother became pregnant. My younger brother's arrival had brought fiery fights between my parents—each argument devolved into an inquisition into the timing of the boy's arrival and the period of their separation. She was getting bigger by the day and probably fed up with yet another pregnancy and the frequent fights with my father.

"I'm gonna have a blond, blue-eyed girl, and we'll throw you in the dumpster we rescued you from," she liked to say to me. The day the baby was born, I hid and peeked into the hospital room where my mother held the very white newborn she had threatened me with. He didn't have blue eyes, but he had my distrust. Here was the threat – the reason that my mother would abandon me.

Back at home, my mother often accused me of putting things in my vagina whenever I took too long in the bathroom. I liked to climb the acacia tree in front of my house and hide seedpods in my underwear to play with later. When she discovered me walking funny, she beat me for putting things in my vagina although I hadn't. I was too young to even understand what she meant.

I was constantly beaten with her belt for the slightest of mistakes. One night, after she viciously attacked me, I fell asleep crying. I woke up to her caressing my head and saying, "I beat you because I love you."

I carry my paternal grandmother on my skin and in my name. Rosa Coiman was a Black woman and a single mother, who gave her name to her two sons. Although stomach cancer took her before I could have direct memories, she is the best of my heritage. I carry her name with pride. After learning about genetics in school, I wondered why my mother had married the son of a Black woman if she didn't like Black people. Of the seven children, I wasn't the blackest. My younger sister was. But her straight hair saved her from my mother's categorization – turd – which she reserved for me alone. When I wrote about these things to Zoë, she would write back saying, "Your mother is a very sick woman."

*

MY MOTHER LIKED to wash my hair with chamomile tea to make it look lighter. As I grew older, my hair grew darker, and my mother and I looked alike. I was darker and slimmer, but we had the same pear-shaped body with small breasts, wide hips, round behinds, and robust legs. Her hair was curly too, but not as tight and unwieldy as mine, which depending on weather and mood, was a battle of ringlets over my forehead, or a high and frizzy afro. She brushed her hair with ease and carried it in relaxed waves.

"I told you to brush your hair! You look like a whore. Look at those negras in the neighborhood. Their hair is twice as bad as yours, and they look tidy. Why don't you brush your hair? ¡Esta muchacha el carajo!" Sometimes she grabbed my hair and smacked my head on the wall.

She asked a neighbor to roll my hair every Saturday. I would sit quietly in the neighbor's porch while she rolled my hair, but it never lasted because I was never taught how to take care of it. No one showed me how to moisturize my curls, preserve them. I didn't know how to wear it "attractively."

When I menstruated for the first time, she took me to a hairdresser and had my hair straightened, like a rite of passage. I returned home, reeking of rotten eggs with bangs falling over my eyes. My brothers stood in front of me mocking, "She went to the witch to have a spell put on her hair. Look at the hair." They laughed, taunting me for hours, until in desperation I ran into the shower to wash the relaxer away, but the hair process was permanent. I was left with wet, straight wire bangs falling across my face. They called me "pelo e' guaya," which means wire hair. I cried and was beaten again for wasting my mother's money. "You were born to be a whore, that's why you don't like straight hair."

*

MY OLDER SIBLINGS learned the gamut of bullying antics from name calling to kicking and punching from my mother long before I was born. By the time I was 12, my brothers had created a whole lexicon of names that enforced my mother's beauty standards and called attention to my physical shortcomings: *Ironing board* for my flat pubescent chest; *Bembona* for my thick lips; *Skier* or *Cinderella's step sister* for my unusually big feet; *Chicharronua* for my kinky hair; *Llorona* for crying easily; *Chismosa* for snitching; *Meona* for my hyperactive bladder; *Cheetah* for my apparent resemblance to Tarzan's beloved chimpanzee. Sometimes in chorus, sometimes in solo, and sometimes in reprimand, my brothers and later, my younger sister, name-called me constantly. Each name fragmented my body, and I felt as segmented as a piece of meat in a butcher shop, tenderized with pounding.

My siblings would put cockroaches in my hands to see how long it took for me to pee in my pants. Once I felt the little monsters crawling on my hands, my out of control bladder released its contents on my pants to their amusement. When my mother hid candy, they would eat the candy and blame it on me. My mother would then ask me, under oath, saying she would fall dead and stiff if I lied, "Did you eat the candy?" She responded to my denials with a shower of beatings for wishing her death. Would I have been punished less severely if I had said yes? I do not know, but I do know I never lied.

The only place I was safe was at Escuela Estatal Simón Rodríguez, where I excelled in my classes. My teachers didn't notice my bruises, but frequently commented on my skills, advanced for my young age, and the small praise was enough to keep my soul intact. "¡Qué bien escribes, niña!" They shared my writing with other teachers, who would then ask my age before praising. Weekdays were easier to handle.

On Sunday nights, my mother's favorite entertainment was to watch horror films broadcast in one of the two available channels on the black and white TV in our living room. I couldn't go to sleep alone while the others watched the movie and its soundtrack echoed through the house. I chose to stay up and endure the horrifying scenes and go to bed only when the film was over.

My brothers waited for me to pull my bed cover over my head and fall asleep. Then they draped their own bed covers over their heads before visiting my bedroom with props like knives or flashlights. They chanted and screeched—whatever satisfied their sadistic needs. I would wake up screaming, sometimes wetting the bed, my bladder unprepared for the fright. My parents would run to the room to see what was going on; then, they scolded me, and laughed at me for being such a wimp. Each time, they dismissed the boys' cruelty as rambunctious, boyish behavior.

Having a regularly sleepless childhood, I saw things floating in my room and inside closets—things that I knew did not exist. The images were elaborate monster cockroaches, bats, headless zombies, ghosts, and an assortment of other creatures. But none of these compared to the nightmare that haunted my sleep. Though I fought to stay awake, eventually my eyes closed. A man dressed in a black hat and a dark suit waited for me outside the house by the acacia tree. He would take me to the cemetery and bury me alive. I would scream muffled sounds and wake up choking. He visited me for years.

*

DRIVING IN THE countryside on long weekend vacations always meant that my father had to stop the car several times to allow me to pee by the side of the road. Sometimes it wasn't possible to pull over. The taunting that followed was unbearable; I would cry, stomp my feet, and beg them to stop, to no avail. When we arrived at our destination, I would get out of the car with my wet pants and my four brothers taunting, "Meona, meona, meona," which means *wetter*, their voices shrill in my ears.

Wetting the bed on a night before school required a private routine. At that time, the water service was irregular; months could go by without us seeing water coming out of the pipes unless my father paid a cistern truck to load the house tank. We also kept big barrels of water in the backyard, which was inhabited by cockroaches at night. I needed to be up at 4:00 a.m. to catch the bus for school. A bad night meant that I had to go down to the dark yard, when only the rooster and my mother were awake, to wash my sheets and wash myself, while she scorned me from above, "Cochina, meona."

The bus commute took two hours before reaching its destination. The school was far away and in the Caracas' red district. My mother considered our hometown school with so many negros a problem for me. My brothers were not in danger; they were male. According to my mother, I could be molested or get pregnant in a school with "those negros." She deemed it safer to put me on a long bus ride with strangers. I suffered from frequent bladder infections, which my mother always attributed to my poor hygiene.

*

AS WE GREW OLDER, my mother and brother's attention to my body shifted and filled with sexual undertones. Mother suggested that I was slutty despite my tomboyishness and preference to do things my brothers did: play baseball, play war, join hide-and-seek, or run wild in the neighboring hills. My younger sister titled me, *Perra.* My older brother, by then a premed student, began calling me *borderline* and enjoyed making me mad just to hear me scream.

My mother declared my adolescent moodiness as hysteria, described in old medical books as an illness related to sexual needs. She told my brothers to stick their fingers inside my vagina as a cure to calm me down, "Métanle el deo', pa'que se le pase."

One of them did stick more than a finger in me. Molestation grew into blunt incest when a fight evolved from horsing around to my brother being on top of me, hard between my legs. I opened the front of my blouse, and we continued clumsily. I didn't lose my virginity then, but it was close. I don't blame my brother. He was only fourteen. I was just twelve. I never said no.

Once, my mother entered my bedroom with her usual accusatory tone, ready to sentence me. She cornered me against the salmon and white lacquered armoire that sheltered me whenever I wanted to cry alone. She threatened me with the four-inch leather belt around her hand and insisted I tell her about a sexual life I didn't know I already had.

"Do you already know man?" she screamed at my face.

"I don't know," I responded, horrified.

Whatever answer I gave her would be the perfect excuse to beat me with the belt. I knew the answer to the question. I had explored sex with my brother, but I had the feeling she didn't want to know that. She was accusing me of something different.

Backing up slowly, I tripped and fell inside the armoire, butt first. My legs went up the moment I fell, and my mother transmuted into a massive cockroach standing in front of me—her legs, now hands, looking for the meeting of my thighs.

"¿Ya conoces macho, coño e'madre?" she asked again as our eyes met. I struggled to comprehend her intentions. What did she want to do now that I was helpless, on my back, inside the armoire? I didn't stay to find out. I closed my eyes and pushed her with both of my feet. She hit the edge of the bed as I pulled myself up and ran out of the bedroom with my mother behind, yelling for me to stop.

My father was always there, somewhere in the house, and never moved a finger to stop the abuse.

*

ONCE MY SON and I started living together in Jussef's apartment, I didn't go to my family's house anymore. Not even when my mother invited Ramón to visit on weekends or insisted on taking him with her on vacation to the house in the Andes. I kept minimal contact with my siblings and my extended family. Even from a distance, I could picture several of my brothers and part of my extended family in my parents' house on a Sunday afternoon. I still felt the burden of their ridicule and mockery and was happy to no longer put up with it.

They gathered in the small front garden where harts tongue, callas and omnipresent roses (the name of my grandmother, my mother, and my sister) adorned the small rectangle of dirt just below the front bedroom windows.

After more than 30 years, my mother's cooking skills had improved a great deal and positioned her as the matriarch of the family among her own siblings. In plain clothes, without makeup or jewelry, my mother enjoyed cooking for her siblings and their spouses, for my father and his brother, and her own brood with their wives and children, who happened to pop by to savor her *sancochos* and cakes.

She kept her children close by being a generous and manipulative giver. She drained her salary to provide for her unemployed adult children or to buy clothes for her grandchildren. She always made sure Los Coimans had food in their refrigerators, and that they came back to her on Sundays to meet with the rest of the clan. They sat on a bench on the porch with the aunts and uncles and cousins, sometimes singing, dándole a la lengua, gossiping about whoever was absent, and drinking beer, rum, or whisky until they became combative with each other.

I sometimes pictured the cake. There would surely be cake because my mother baked the best—something she learned from her own abusive mother, the one who also raised seven children after her alcoholic husband went to jail on charges of conspiracy to overthrow the government about half a century before.

My mother baked elaborate confections with entire circus tents and clowns on trapeze, or Southern belles with their long fluffy dresses falling in cascades, or race car tracks with tiny Hot Wheels. She never charged a cent for the fantasy scene cakes she made for friends and family alike, and we always enjoyed them, casually for dinner, or more formally for a party. From the moist bread pudding soaked in rum that she would put together during the week, to the intricate ensembles she decorated for hours before a baptism or a birthday, her cakes filled the house with the sweetness of vanilla and buttered sugar. We competed for the pleasure of licking the mixing bowl, or the wooden spoon, or eating the pieces of cake crust she shaved off the cake before decorating it. She was good at it. She baked for the privilege of gathering the family on Sundays and holidays. Even though we knew she enjoyed having the entire family around her, she always complained about the burden of cooking for so many people and never having a Sunday off.

I grieved the loss of my tribe and Sunday gatherings with my cousins, aunts and uncles, but I decided that to break from my mother, I needed to break away from it all. It was the beginning of a deep isolation, but I didn't know it then.

*

I FELT OBLIGATED to show up at Jussef's family's house every Sunday. Lunch was served by early afternoon in the formal dining room, where the table was fully dressed with embroidered linen and silverware. The women and servants paraded elaborate dishes from the kitchen to the table: baked kibbeh, stuffed grape leaves, stuffed zucchini and meat rolls, all delicacies from the gastronomic paradise that was Aleppo, Syria. They placed the food at the center of the table while the conversation shifted from praising the food to commenting on others not present. When they had eaten enough of the main course, the women stood up, taking turns to collect the dirty dishes and bring out fruit. Later, they moved to the family room. The smaller space, decorated with fresh rattan furniture, opened up to a courtyard with a pomegranate tree at its center. There, Jussef's family continued the conversation over dessert and coffee, as visitors came in and out of the house in a constant stream of faces under heavy makeup, speaking Arabic.

Turkish coffee served in tiny cups passed from one hand to another. When the coffee finished, cups were turned over onto their saucers and twirled three times, left waiting for the grounds to fall. The ritual of reading the coffee grounds involved several more hours of nibbling on chocolate candy, nuts, and other treats. By 6 p.m., I was bloated and sick of the passive aggressive comments from my mother-in-law and sister-in-law.

"I have a bag of clothes I no longer use. Do you want to take it to your family, Lisbeth? I am sure somebody there will need it," my mother-in-law said.

There wasn't much difference between our two families. Both gathered frequently and exuded similar toxicity: who dressed better, who cooked better, who was dating a loser, who said what about whom. I didn't see the difference between the two families, only that there was more money here, and the Arab food was great. During the many social events, Arabic surrounded me and stabbed my ears with the strength of rejection. From time to time, the women eyed me from top to bottom and commented to one another, their heads close together. I felt excluded while I sat at their table, thinking about Jussef and I having sex in the little apartment on Torre Andrés Bello.

His mother became a constant presence in our lives, much to my chagrin. A penitence I had to endure for defying my own mother, I thought. Jussef's mom was an excellent cook and loved gardening and crafting; both women were equally manipulative and drama connoisseurs.

Jussef's mother also did not like my skin color, which she referred to as "criollita."

"Mira, Jussef, she is so criollita. Couldn't you find anybody better?" she'd ask him.

"I like criollita," Jussef said.

That was before she learned I was a single mother. Then she lashed out about honor, the reputation of the family and whatnot.

After these gatherings, we drove back home in the Lada. Jussef drove while Ramón slept in the back seat, and I regurgitated kibbeh. I thought his mother was trying to poison me with her food. It hurt so badly that sometimes we had to stop along the way for me to throw up.

Choices Made

"DO YOU WANT to go play with your friend Edward?" I asked Ramón one March afternoon in the round apartment on Avenida Andrés Bello. Jussef stood at the balcony, peeling my clothes off with his eyes.

"Yes. Can you call his mom?"

"Of course," I said while grabbing the phone. "Can Ramón come down to play with Edward? OK?" With the phone at my ear, I flirted with Jussef, silently asking him to wait for me while I made our encounter happen.

"She said you can go now. She will call me to pick you up in about two hours. Pick up your toys from the floor before you leave," I told Ramón while trying to hide my enthusiasm at his play date. We took every opportunity to have Ramón go out on a play date or stay with a babysitter.

Sometimes we just sent him to run short errands, and as soon as he was out the door, Jussef would grab me by the waist, pull me closer to him, kiss me on the neck, pull my hair down firmly, and then bend down over my breast, while I stripped my shirt and bra off.

He kissed the sides of my breasts and then sucked on my nipples. At the same time, his hands pushed my panties away, and his fingers played with my clitoris. I begged him to fuck me, to eat me alive, to never stop, reciprocating the pleasure I received with biting kisses, stripping his clothes off, moaning with desire. I dropped on my knees and satisfied him, savoring his penis with my tongue, sucking and sliding up and down, while my hands grabbed his buttocks or played with his testicles. Then he stood up, ran to get a condom as if he was running to save his life. I stood, feeling the memory of his hands over my body, relishing the view of El Avila in front of me. When he was ready, he pushed me against the cold door, his thighs pressed against mine, penetrating me with a fire between his legs that could ignite a gas stove. I laced my legs around his waist to let him in, holding my body between the door and his torso, dripping with lust, and thirsty for more. When he got tired of holding me on his waist, he put me down, turned me around, and we fucked like horses. I stepped on the clothes lying on the shiny granite floor in disarray, my long and robust legs holding us in our frenetic exchange of orgasms. In the height of our ecstasy, I saw myself on the back of a winged horse, gliding above Caracas' sky.

No wonder I got pregnant.

Well into my undergraduate program, I was not ready to exchange a degree for a pregnancy, even when I had conceived with a man I was deeply in love with.

Jussef went with me to the clinic for the procedure. A regular ob/gyn office was the cathartic place where women display their feminine endurance: who had suffered the worst birth pain, and whose endometriosis had caused more bleeding, among other horrific conversation topics. Instead, an eerie quietness weighed heavy as an anvil over the waiting room inside the abortion clinic, a non-descriptive medical office in a tall medical building in the northern part of the city.

We all knew what the other was doing in the well-lit waiting room, where we five or six women busied ourselves with the cat's hair on our blouses, or peeled the polish off our nails, or curled our hair with playful fingers. One woman took out a little pocket mirror and retouched her lips. Jussef and I talked in whispers, as though attending a funeral and needing to go to the bathroom in the middle of the service. Nobody made casual comments about the weather. We treated each other as anonymous criminals. Bonded by the pain of a lonely and controversial decision, we sentenced ourselves to never look into each other's eyes, nor share a smile or a trivial comment.

When it was time to register and pay, Jussef stood up and wrote the check. He held me tight when my name was called. Abortion was not and is not legal in Venezuela, but it's common and mostly safe if you can pay for it. I was lucky we could afford a good service.

Inside the outpatient surgery room, I was handed a few forms to complete my medical history. One question stood out: Reason for requesting an abortion. I said I didn't want another baby at the moment. There was no risk in this pregnancy. I was not destitute, and the pregnancy had been a product of love. Yet, I didn't want another baby at the moment and wasn't having one.

Then, I lay on the examination table, my legs spread apart on the stirrups, and a cannula in my right wrist, a bright light directed between my legs.

"We will first apply local anesthesia. Then we will insert this, you see? It looks like a wand, but it's actually a vacuum. It works with manual suction and it's fast. It'll be over in less than ten minutes. Do you have any questions?" the young doctor asked as the nurse injected the IV through the cannula.

"I'm fine," I said on the verge of tears.

"Now we want you to relax as much as you can." The nurse spoke to me in a soothing tone and held my hand for comfort.

I looked up into the void and saw a yellow smiley face sticker on the ceiling. A note under the smiley face read, "I know what you are going through." I had an abortion and somebody understood that it wasn't easy, that I needed support, that I hated the silence in the waiting room.

Jussef waited outside. When it was over, we exited the building without speaking. Once in the courtyard, we hugged for a long time.

*

WITH MAPS, our suitcases, and borrowed winter coats in our hands, we waited at Archer Station for the subway to Manhattan. We had gone to New York to visit Zoë for Christmas. Before leaving, a judge gave us permission to travel with my son because the biological father was nowhere to be found. We added those documents to the adoption file.

Zoë lived in Manhattan, in the Upper West Side, close to Columbia University. She offered her home and hosted a Christmas dinner for the three of us, and her boyfriend at the time. She put a turkey in the oven, opened a can of cranberry sauce and a bag of precooked green beans, and served salad from a supermarket ready box. She laughed as she cut the turkey and said she was introducing us to a typical American Christmas dinner. In a photo of her that evening, she can be seen holding a butcher knife, psycho style, close to her boyfriend's neck. "I am going to cut the turkey," I remember her joking.

For his Christmas present, Ramón asked if we could take him to the Natural History Museum. There were real dinosaur fossils he wanted to see. We satisfied his scientific curiosity, and after that I took him to a park near Zoë's apartment so he could learn to roller skate. It was like watching a baby deer take its first steps. He fell and fell, and I lifted him up until he was able to hold ground and skate alone. Jussef chose to bail out and visit the Metropolitan Museum alone. The next day, when we did go out together, he was relentless, wanting to rest just enough to go out again and see more, even though my feet were killing me.

"I don't like Jussef," Zoë said. "He wears you out, he is too hard on you."

"There is no other way to explore a foreign city in so few days." I excused him.

I saw a bit of her life in the short time we were there. She had an office in the back of her apartment, where she ran her small and successful business, "Creative Medical Communications." Although she was Jewish, she had the entire apartment decorated for Christmas and made sure there were Christmas presents for all the kids she knew and loved, and there were many. Her friends' children, whom she helped raise and care for, all were a fundamental part of her life.

In the afternoons, after she finished working and had chatted with us a bit, she went out with her friends to give us space. When I tried to clean her apartment as a way of saying thank you for her hospitality, she got really mad and ushered us out of the house, encouraging us to discover the city.

The crisp air of New York in winter smelled of roasted nuts and chocolate cookies. I carried the scent with me in my hair and clothes as I boarded the plane back home, and it stayed even as I opened my suitcases in Caracas. I unpacked the books I needed for my research on Sonia Sanchez. Zoë wanted to help me out with the books, so at her request, I left her a list she could buy for me and send by mail. I didn't miss New York, but I missed the opportunity to dream a life for myself – the life Zoë was living.

Months later a letter in the mail brought news of Zoë's broken heart.

> 3/27/95
>
> I can't tell you how much I miss _____. Everyday I have to stop myself from dialing his number and asking him to come back – or at least spend the night with me. I know from a friend that he is already dating some young, beautiful woman, and is extremely happy with his new life. Somehow that only makes it feel worse.
>
> I have forced myself to go out and start dating new people, but none of them really fill the bill. It's a sad assortment of

> guys, and really nobody appropriate for me. So I'll just keep looking and try to work on developing other interest and more a sense of who I am and what I want.

*

AFTER GOING DOWN the long stairs of the court building, we stepped onto the busy street in downtown Caracas.

"I can't believe I've been court ordered to marry you," Jussef said.

"Don't be dramatic," I replied.

"Look who's talking about drama," he joked.

As the completion of my thesis approached and our talks about emigration abounded, we chose to accelerate the procedures to finalize Jussef's adoption of my son. When everything had fallen into place and all requirements had been met, we faced the judge in the final adoption hearing, where he declined, on the argument that he couldn't grant adoption rights to a single man. His advice was for marrying the mother. "You will have full parental rights over the child then," the judge said. We agreed that it was a practical decision.

Later, I sat across from a couple of classmates at the school cafeteria. I told them the news to survey their opinion.

"I don't need to marry him. We can live together forever, and I wouldn't have to put up with his mom. But it would mean the world to Ramón. I'm confused, I don't know what to do," I told them.

"Marry him," said the older. "You don't have anything to lose, and it's the best for your son."

"I wouldn't," said the younger. "You are not going to be happy if you don't marry for true love."

"I'm in love, but I just don't feel the need to marry," I replied.

I thought back to all Jussef had done for Ramón and me.

When a doctor had said the child needed to have his tonsils and adenoids removed, Jussef paid for the surgery and sat by my side in the waiting room, holding my hand. He paid for Ramón's education in the Catholic school, took him to the movies when I needed a break, listened to him play his violin, and read to him when I was too busy with schoolwork.

I couldn't wait for a letter to deliver the news to my friend. So I called Zoë to tell her about the fast approaching adoption.

Zoë was happy for me despite her feelings for Jussef.

"Yeeeah," she said in a cheerleader tone. "When is the wedding?"

"It's not a wedding," I replied. "We just have to go to the judge, bring a couple of witnesses who can testify that we have lived together for over six years. Then the judge will say that we are a married couple and that Jussef takes Ramón as his son. We will have a marriage license and the adoption sentence in one single act. We will then take the adoption sentence to the register to have the new birth certificate made for Ramón."

"I say you are trying to make it sound detached and bureaucratic and deny the emotional importance it has for you. You are getting married. Enjoy it," Zoë encouraged.

"It's not that important for me. It's important for Ramón," I insisted.

"Oh, come on, Lisbeth," continued Zoë. "You're bullshitting yourself. You have been living a torrid and rocky relationship with Jussef for eight years. He's defied his mother and his family. You've made changes to stay with him – sold your apartment, moved to Caracas, went back to college, and now you are making it look as if it's just a stupid paper."

"No, really, it's nothing." I almost cried.

"Suit yourself," she said and hung up.

Jussef sat across from me in the formal living room of his cousin's house. Ramón played nearby. The house offered all the details of the Syrian home I had learned to recognize: the wooden boxes decorated in geometrical patterns in mother-of-pearl, brass plates with inscriptions in Arabic, polished granite floors, and an ample and well equipped kitchen that seemed to burst with life.

Jussef cousin helped us expedite the marriage paperwork, including a prenuptial agreement.

"He doesn't want me to murder him and run away with the money," I said.

"Not funny. I need a list of your assets," she told me.

"I don't have any. I used to have an apartment and sold it. I broke even. Didn't make any money from it."

"Just give me a bank account number so that I can list that as your assets."

"No. I came to this relationship with nothing, and if I have to leave, will do so empty handed."

"Whatever you say," she said.

I hid my resentment. I didn't have my own lawyer cousin to protect me against the unbalanced deal I signed into.

*

ON THE MORNING OF November 24, 1995, Jussef went to work and I went to school as usual. The day before, I had gone to the salon to tidy my hair and do my nails. After picking up Ramón from school, I went home to change clothes. I wore a two-piece set: a short flower print skirt and a beige blouse with rosette buttons. I wore pearl earrings and a matching necklace. Ramón dressed in his violin recital outfit - navy blue pants, white shirt, and black shoes - and we drove the little Lada at an insane speed to get to downtown on time. There wasn't a single parking space, so I finally threw the keys at the valet, shouting from the other side of the car, "I am getting married! I'll be back in two hours!" and ran down the street with Ramón jogging by my side to the tribunal building on the corner of Cruz Verde and Camejo, hoping my high heels wouldn't break in the effort.

Jussef waited for me in his linen suit and his round glasses. Eunice's husband, Edgar stood as a witness. We recruited a court clerk to stand for us as the second witness before the judge. The judge pronounced us husband and wife, and Jussef slid the gold band on my right ring finger as it is the custom for civil unions in Venezuela. I took my glasses off, and we kissed. Ramón beamed, clapping his skinny hands in joy. A broad smile lit his eyes behind his little glasses. I was so happy for him and wished I could hold onto that moment for him.

We walked hand-in-hand to the nearby Catedral de Caracas and into the Museo Sacro, where a little restaurant with ancient brick walls and hanging flower baskets was located. We had sandwiches and batidos for lunch, a simple banquet for such an important event. That evening, several friends from college and a few neighbors showed up at our apartment to celebrate and posed as our angry parents in the mock "official" wedding pictures.

Jussef's younger brother, Jamil, also came by. I had gone to the tiny kitchen to serve some drinks for my friends, when he found me there alone. I was beaming with joy and thanked him for showing up. "It means so much to me that you are here. I know Jussef must have told his family unofficially, but I didn't expect any of you to come," I said.

My friend Marianella came in the kitchen looking for a beer and interrupted our conversation. Jamil busied himself, looking for ice in the refrigerator, watching the city lights from the kitchen window. When she exited the kitchen, and he was sure we were alone, he delivered this line: "I wish Jussef had chosen something better, but I congratulate you for your success."

I thanked him with a half smile. "Now, please excuse me. I have to bring this beer to my friend. It's already warming up." I was quickly becoming skilled at hiding disappointment and anger.

In the living room, the soft sound of sparkling wine being poured into glasses, laughter and conversation from my friends, and Ramón's bright smile reminded me that we had great reasons to celebrate. We were a family now, a funny family who all wore glasses – the skinny boy with round eyes like a Japanese anime character, the mom with a scar, and the father who part-timed as Pegasus on our wild nights.

Landed Immigrants

ON OCCASION ZOË and I talked for an hour or so over the phone, quickly catching up on the events in each other's lives.

"I want to have a baby before I grow too old," she said once, "but most of my friends think I'm crazy."

"I don't think you're crazy. You've done everything you want with your life, but if you feel a child is what you are missing, you should go for it. If you don't, I'm afraid you'll grow old with regret."

"The adoption process can take years. I don't have that kind of time."

"What do you think of surrogacy?" I asked.

"I like the idea, but I'll have to find somebody I really trust. Would you do it?"

"Wait. I wasn't thinking about myself." With my face resting on my left hand, I quickly thought of the possibility. Zoë was my best friend, and I really wanted to help her find a baby. "I was just suggesting it, but if I do, I'd need to see the baby grow. Would you allow me to do so?"

"No, Lisbeth. If you accept, we wouldn't see each other again," she said.

"I can't do that, Zoë. I could never be away from a baby I carry to term. But I'm going to help you look for adoption opportunities here in Venezuela," I said.

Zoë chose not to find a surrogate and initiate her adoption search. But she had to be warned.

"Zoë, for the first time in your life, be selfish, will you?"

Even though Zoë was a strong woman, she had the tendency of investing herself in relationships where children were involved. Zoë's involvement in my life proved her altruism knew no boundaries. The only reason I found for her to pour herself so much to our relationship was my own son. She helped the child by helping the mother. And I was sure Ramón and I were not the only beneficiaries of her generosity. For the first time since we met, she was trying to help herself, not others, and it was difficult.

"The woman I was hoping would give me her baby for adoption has been running a fever. And she lied to me about it," Zoë said on the phone.

"Does she have a cold?" I asked.

"No. It seems that she has an infection of sorts, and it's an ongoing problem," she said and broke down crying.

"That can't be good, dear. I say walk out. You are not doing social work. Think of you first, would you? Do everything you can to provide well for the expecting mother. Make sure she has excellent prenatal care, is well fed, and has all her needs covered. But you are not going to take care of a sick, pregnant woman. If she lied, let her deal with it."

"I had so many expectations," she said, sobbing.

"But it's not a good match, sweetheart."

Weeks passed without hearing from her, until she called again one evening.

"I got news for you," she said.

"A boyfriend?"

"No. An expectant mother."

We both screamed.

"I want to hug you. I'm so happy for you," I said when we calmed down. I was so happy for my friend. She had everything she wished for. I wanted to celebrate with her, treat her to dinner or drinks, and perhaps organize a baby shower. But none of that was within reach. I could only cheer for her over the phone.

"But now I'm afraid. What if I am not a good mother?" she said. Again, I heard the need for reassurance.

"Zoë, you'll be a great mother. I know. You've been a mother to me, and you are the best."

A couple of weeks later, I announced to her my own pregnancy.

After Jussef's adoption of Ramón was finalized, Jussef and I decided to have another child. I felt serene and happy although I was in the last stretch of finishing my undergraduate thesis.

"I wish our babies would get to know each other," I said.

"You are the only one who is encouraging me through this," she said.

"That's hard to believe. You have a very supportive group of friends."

"Yes, but they don't agree," Zoë said.

"I think it's your insecurities speaking. You want to have approval, and they have reservations. You'll be fine. Trust yourself, and they will trust you," I said.

*

ON GRADUATION NIGHT, Jussef and I danced the macarena. We looked at each other and smiled as we played the sequence of arm movements, wishing to give our bodies some joy. When it was my turn to place my hands on my behind, I reached behind my bloated body and stopped. Thirty-six weeks pregnant and suffocating, I held my lower back with my hands and wobbled past the dancers to the chair closest to the buffet. I decided not to attend the commencement ceremony at Universidad Metropolitana. I imagined I'd look like a tent inside the black cap and gown outfit. This graduation party at a friend's house was my only celebration. I sat on the chair and reached over for the colorful and tasty hors d'oeuvre to stuff myself with prosciutto, fruit, and cake.

In a country without reliable postal service, a private express letter delivered wished-for but unexpected news. A letter from the Canadian embassy instructed us to undergo a thorough medical evaluation to complete our immigration process.

A year ago, when Jussef told his mother we had married, he grew concerned about the family dynamics if his mother refused to accept my son and me. That night, he came back home and asked for the Canadian application for immigration I had shown him so many times. He filled it out and shortly after, we received the results. We were eligible for landed immigrant status, the equivalent of an American green card. While I was writing my thesis and growing a baby inside of me, Jussef fed Ramón a diet of fast food and took care of the immigration procedures.

As directed, Jussef and Ramón went to the doctor, but I had to wait until after the baby was born. So I went to the dermatologist to ask for a written explanation of my rare skin condition, and to the ob/gyn for a copy of my medical history to get ready for the physical exam.

When I went for a sonogram, just before the baby was born, Jussef and Ramón asked to be present. Although I secretly wanted to have a girl, I preferred for it to be a surprise. We had decorated a corner of our bedroom in gender-neutral yellow and green and bought matching bedding and clothing. We had two names ready: Nourel for a girl, and Saul for a boy. In went the three of us into the sonogram room, Jussef on one side and Ramón on the other side of the bed. The doctor was explaining positions and crowning, when suddenly Ramón yelled out, "It's a boy! I can see his pee-pee."

We welcomed Saul on November 11, 1996. The private clinic was within a walking distance from our apartment. Ramón refused to go to school that day not wanting to miss the event.

Wide-awake with partial anesthesia for a C-section, I felt the pressure as the baby was pulled from my womb. I cried from overwhelming emotion when the nurse put the baby on my chest. "Te llamas Saul. Bienvenido al mundo," I said.

He was covered in gooey white film, slimy and bloody. I touched his head ever so slightly as tears rolled down my face. Those were the only peaceful moments we had for the next few days. He was immediately whisked away to the incubator, the standard procedure at that time. Jussef was not allowed into the delivery room.

My tubes were tied as per my instructions. At 32, I was happy to be a mother again, but sure I didn't want any more children. My husband and I had talked about it, and I gave him the choice: "Either you have a vasectomy, or I tie my tubes."

Outside the delivery room, my family had gathered. I passed by them as the nurse wheeled me to the recovery room. Ramón, a skinny 11-year-old, smiled and fidgeted while Jussef paced the corridor. My mother and father – humbly dressed and hating each other – stood on the opposite side of the hall across from my mother-in-law, who eyed them from over her shoulder. My parents and Jussef's family had never met before. We knew there wasn't any point in it.

While in recovery, I could smell my foul breath and felt pain every time I tried to move. My college classmates came to meet the baby and brought presents with them, but I couldn't bring myself to be friendly. I felt sticky and uncomfortable and wished somebody was kind enough to help me take a shower or brush my teeth.

"You are the king, and nobody will replace you. You understand?" my mother told Ramón in an audible whisper. Though they had gathered in the hall, I could hear every word.

"You have to understand that Saul is now the most important person in the world," my mother-in-law told Ramón.

Later, Eunice helped the nurse clean me up.

Zoë's child was born a few weeks later. She was overjoyed with a sense of fulfillment. She had achieved everything she ever wanted professionally and personally, and now life had granted her a child. Our correspondence evolved into periodic emails. With the excitement of the baby, the timbre of her letters changed. With a baby in her arms, she now wrote emails about diaper rash, meeting schedules and finding reliable babysitters. I no longer imagined her as a demigoddess sitting at the top of Mount Olympus. Rather she now sounded real, like me, with problems similar to mine, negotiating her routine around baby bottles and scheduled check-ups at the pediatrician's office. I wanted to hug her and share with her our beautiful mother moments, but it wasn't possible. All we could do was talk on the phone or write emails when we were not too tired. In those moments, I learned about her life with her gorgeous baby, and how the baby had only a sparse fluff of hair.

"What color is her hair?" I asked

"Dirty blonde," she wrote back.

Ramón and Jussef were infatuated with Saul. They couldn't wait to come home to bathe him, play with him, and teach him tricks. "See what he can do now, Mamá," said Ramón from time to time and showed me how the baby could turn or smile at the sound of something familiar, or how he stuck his tongue out.

Jussef impressed me. Where he had been detached and cerebral with Ramón, he was now an affectionate homebody. I shuddered with tenderness looking at him with the baby in the dim corner of our bedroom. It was a father-son bonding that I had never seen before or since. He called dibs on the last feeding of the night, which I had to prepare a bottle of my milk for. Jussef sat on the rocking chair and undressed from the waist up. With the moonlight shining over them through the window, he cooed over the little thing against his hairy chest. He fed the baby his last meal of the day, touching the baby's head with his long, aquiline nose. Maybe it was Jussef's attention, but that baby slept all night long since he was one month old.

I felt my heart expanding with the baby and my little family's newfound tenderness. Jussef and I didn't fight anymore. We were ready to fully accommodate each other. Jussef took pictures all the time. He snapped a photo of Ramón sitting on the couch holding the baby, or of the four of us, all bespectacled except for baby Saul. We all wondered if Saul too would wear glasses one day and how he would look with spectacles among so much hair and thick eyebrows.

*

WHEN OUR RELATIVES entered the picture, things were not as sublime. Jussef's family especially brought tension since I was able to keep my own family at bay. Even though Saul was only a few weeks old, I managed to decorate the apartment for Christmas, bought presents for everyone and invited his family over for New Year's Eve. I served mostly store-bought finger foods, fine cheeses, dips, and fruit.

"I wouldn't serve visitors anything I hadn't cooked myself," Jussef's mother nitpicked from behind her drink.

With the possibility of moving to Canada in the air, and a low maintenance baby, little by little, I developed a reliable routine that included time with friends. We had been in our apartment for eight years and had a strong group of friends among our neighbors who happily doubled as babysitters. From time to time, we could go on an evening date although we rarely found the energy to do so. I made swim dates with friends and their babies. Ramón's friends from school, and Jussef's friends from work visited us. I felt much better engaging with others after Saul was born.

Life slowed down considerably. It was a nice break from my last year in college, when I had written my thesis and had run like a headless chicken to meet the graduation deadlines. I soon started feeling I needed something else beyond the baby's sweetness. I heard about a faculty position opening up at my former school. I initiated conversations to apply to teach Introduction to Literature. I could picture myself as a college professor. I just heard about the possibility, but never actually initiated the application process or had a job offer.

*

SOMETIME IN MID April 1997, express mail delivered a notice about our Canadian Landed Immigrant status. I pulled out a thick envelope from the sealed package and squealed when I saw the Canadian Embassy address. Jussef pulled out his glasses, rubbed his eyes, and slid his hands slowly over his balding head. I could see the torment he felt over the decision he had to make. I relished the moment. The idea of a life without my mother or mother-in-law excited me. The prospect of safety on the streets, of parks where my children could play free, of a bright future for them filled me with joyful hope.

"Don't say anything yet to anybody. Let's wait a little longer." That was usually Jussef's approach to breaking news. He always needed to wait until the moment was just right. Maybe he needed to think it over, to see if he would change his mind.

In our living room, overlooking El Avila, I broke the news to my skinny son. "Ramón, nos vamos pa' Canadá. But you can't tell anybody yet. Jussef needs a little more time. Our secret. OK?"

"Ok, Mom." But he couldn't hide his excitement. His eyes beamed and danced with joy.

The instructions commanded us to leave immediately. We had until mid July to arrive in Canada as immigrants, or lose the status. We decided Jussef would leave first, rent an apartment, and prepare the way for the children and me. We wrote a to-do list to close our lives in Venezuela for good. The list was a mile long, and I felt as if the floor shook under my feet. I felt unbalanced, with too much to do and too little time. We couldn't count on our families to help since we were keeping the news to ourselves, and our friends could not be recruited. It was Jussef and I, and it was overwhelming.

As I sat in the rocking chair in the bedroom to breastfeed the baby, I pondered what one needed to take to start a life from scratch. Every small decision was a final one. Should I pack the violin even if Ramón didn't play anymore?

We broke the news to Jussef's family in April during one of the extended Sunday lunches. I broke the news to my mother over the phone. "I always knew you'd leave," she said.

My stress escalated when Jussef left in early June. People came in and out of my apartment buying our belongings. Without Jussef to keep them at bay, our mothers increased the pressure. Mine was devastated. The woman who had never said "I love you," now cried at the thought of my departure. Jussef's mother wanted me to visit her house with the baby, although I couldn't find a moment of respite.

Jamil, Jussef's younger brother, called one day. I hated Jussef's mother for the regular harassment, but I still had some good feelings for Jamil. I didn't hesitate taking his call.

"Lisbeth, I want to see Saul," he said. He sounded a bit authoritarian, almost demanding rather than asking.

"I am really busy. I don't have time."

"We are worried that Ramón could hurt little Saul. You know because they are just half brothers." I paused on my side of the line, pondering how to react to this new attack.

"You know what? I don't want to see you anymore, Jamil," I said.

"But you said I was welcome in your house anytime," he said.

"That was before all this. Thank you for your concern. Bye." I slammed the receiver on the phone. "AGGG. Esta gente me tiene harta," I said.

In the middle of all this, an old friend from high school, who was now a well-known radio host, called to interview me on the issue of immigration and the reasons why people left a country like Venezuela. The call came one morning, and I decided to go ahead with the interview, even as people were walking into my place and taking things with them. I gave my opinion. The last words I heard from my friend were: "Well, we just heard Lisbeth Coiman, who spoke so eloquently about the reasons she has to leave the country." But I never heard the end of the segment because soon a buyer looking for a cheap bargain took the radio.

Looking back, my last weeks in Venezuela come to me in flashes: our books packed in boxes, Ramón's violin, a coffee table. I see my family gathered in my parents' house to say goodbye, my nephew Jorge begging me to take him with me and me hugging him and crying. I see Jussef's mother and my friends in the now bare apartment, the cylindrical silhouette of Torre Andrés Bello against the dark silhouette of El Avila in the early hours of the day. I hear the guacharacas' rhythmic call in the distance as a cab takes my children and me to the airport.

Load of Hope

OUR EMBRACE SMELLED of uncertainty. We found a cart to tote our six suitcases, the maximum allowed. With most of our belongings gone, we packed clothes, underwear, shoes, toiletries, some jewelry, and baby things. We also brought our savings and the money we collected from the sale of our cars. It wasn't much, but it was enough to soften the landing. Thirty-four boxes of books would follow via cargo.

"Landed Immigrants?" an official-looking man asked us as soon as we passed through customs.

"Yes. Landed Immigrants."

"Welcome to Canada." He shook our hands with a smile. "Please, follow me." He then directed us to the welcome lounge, where a wall of pamphlets in every imaginable language displayed instructions on how to be a Canadian: how to obtain a driver's license, how to apply for a health card, and for a social security number. When the welcoming officer noticed our baby, he gave us pamphlets on how to use car seats and when to vaccinate. He gave us instructions on how to dress for winter and pamphlets on diversity and multiculturalism. We were welcomed, at least officially.

On July 7, 1997, we walked through the glass doors of Pearson International Airport in Toronto into the first day of our new lives as landed immigrants in Canada.

"I had a hard time finding a rental without any references." Jussef chuckled nervously, his thick eyebrows framing the sadness in his eyes.

The smell of bug killer hit my nose at the apartment door. I immediately felt hundreds of insect legs crawling up my body, and stomped my feet a few times hard on the floor, as if shaking them off me, but there was nothing in on my legs. Just the smell in the air. In a panic, I turned to him and asked, "Are there cockroaches here?"

"Not cockroaches, just roaches. Tiny ones. A lot." He gave me an apologetic smile with his thick round eyebrows raised high, like a kid who has just farted at the dinner table.

It had been a long trip, and I had a baby to feed. Except for the roaches and the mattress on the floor, the apartment was bare. I opened one of the suitcases and took out a pair of sheets and some towels. That night, the four of us slept on the mattress on the floor. We had nothing but the hope that leaving behind all that was familiar, and starting new in a foreign land on a balmy 55° F summer afternoon, was the right decision.

*

FROM OUR 16TH FLOOR apartment on Sherobee Road, we could see the Mississauga Hospital. The high rise reminded me of government housing back home. The apartment had a long balcony with a low veranda, which was a safety hazard for the kids. I worked to keep the parquet floors of the apartment clean so Saul could crawl around inside.

In the afternoons, I explored the neighborhood with the kids. We located two parks just a few blocks away from the intersection of Hurontario and Dundas, where major road expansion was taking place. Bus stops, supermarkets, pharmacies, and walk-in clinics served the neighborhood. A large open space with green turf and tall pine trees protected our building from the noise on Hurontario. Tennis courts bordered one side of the building, while another nicer looking apartment complex sat across the street on Sherobee Road. In the coming fall, Ramón would attend Camilla School, a few blocks away.

The Monday after our arrival, as instructed by the immigration officer at the airport, we applied for our Health and Social Insurance cards. The Health and Social Insurance cards arrived in the mail soon after, but we had to take tests for the difficult-to-obtain driver's license. We waited until late summer to register Ramón for school.

The moving truck arrived the second week. The movers were instructed to unpack and take the empty boxes with them. Now, we had plenty to read and nowhere to sit. Little Saul chewed on the books and climbed on them. We bought a swing that we hung from a doorframe and that helped keep him busy. Ramón, who grew up in Caracas, where children didn't run free or play in the parks, made friends right away. He knew some English already and started speaking in no time and explored the neighborhood, riding his bicycle, happy to be free.

We often ran into people who spoke English with an accent like us. I wondered what a real Canadian looked or sounded like. I didn't understand that we were all real Canadians. We all seemed to have arrived recently, to be in transition, to have a story, to be looking for jobs, and to have doubts about our decisions. We all seemed poor and unbalanced, stressed out, and too concerned about money. As for my little family, although we slept on the floor and ate fast food for two weeks, we were not poor or destitute. We chose this life. Unlike entrenched poverty, immigration inspired hope.

Leaving behind all we had meant building our lives from scratch and buying everything we needed on the cheap. During the day, I wrote what I needed on a list: oil, sugar, flower, pepper, knife, plastic container for leftovers, bathroom mat, and toilet cleaner. While Jussef looked for a job, I did my best to cook our meals with our limited resources. I grew tired of it and came to loathe it, but all beginnings are hard. I told myself there was no reason to complain because it was better than Venezuela.

When shopping, I used my son's stroller to carry items around. I soon learned that this was a mistake.

"Lady? Can you please open your purse?" said a woman with a photo ID hanging from a lanyard across her chest.

"Of course." I complied without hesitation and wondered what had I done

Department stores overwhelmed me because it was too easy to get lost looking for an item, or even for the exit. We were in a department store looking at clothes on a round rack. I turned and lost sight of Saul, who crawled away from me as if he were playing. I finally caught him and sat him back in the stroller. A woman with a walkie-talkie on her belt stopped me and asked me to lift Saul from his seat to check for stolen merchandise. I felt embarrassed and exhausted.

Another day, I was leaving the local Walmart with a huge load of plastic containers and storage organizers in the stroller when a team of two came up to me.

"Miss, can I see your receipt?" said one.

They wore blue polyester uniforms and had lanyards with photo IDs.

"Of course," I pulled out the long bill I had just paid.

"Do you mind if we count each item?"

"Well, I do mind, but I am guessing you are going to count anyway," I replied in an aggravated tone, as I noticed a small circle of curious passersby beginning to form around us.

The women went on counting and scratching them from the list, one by one. I had just spent near CAN$300. There were a lot of small items.

"You are fine. I apologize for the inconvenience. You can go," said the taller of the two women.

I felt humiliated and rushed to the bus stop with tears running down my face and acid in my veins. By that time, Saul was hungry, but before I reached my destination, I had calmed down by focusing my attention on my little son.

On our walks through the neighborhood, I learned about garage sales and began to frequent them on foot with the stroller. My friend Carol Sigurdson, whom I had met while working at the Caracas Hilton many years before, told me over the phone about thrift stores, and I went there too. The shopping spree continued. I came home loaded with mismatched objects: a lamp, a white desk for the computer, a chair for the desk, toys for the boys, containers for the kitchen, a mirror, and a television.

Jussef and I talked about it, and we agreed, "One day we will look back at all this and laugh."

*

OUR CONVERSATIONS ON job rejections kept us awake at night. At first we tried to stay calm for the children's sake. We talked in hushed voices while lying on the mattress and staring at the ceiling. However, by the end of our second month in Canada, the tone of our conversations had changed to confrontation.

"You are being too picky. I want to go back to school," I yelled.

"You want me to throw my career in the garbage," he said as he slammed the bedroom door behind him. The first lesson we had to learn was humility.

Jussef didn't know rejection. Right out of college, when he still had hair on his head, he landed his first and only job at a state of the art oil research institute, subsidiary of the Venezuelan government owned oil company, PDVSA.

I dreamed of graduate school and becoming a college professor. My dreams came crashing sooner than Jussef's. An academic position required a Ph.D. He wouldn't hear of it. My next bet was teaching in a high school, but I needed Canadian certification, and the process would take at least two years, if I was lucky.

"Why don't you accept the scholarship they offered you in Edmonton? I could apply to a graduate program, and we could live as graduate students for a while. After, both of us can get good jobs."

"That sounds very romantic, Lisbeth, but I don't think I can give my children the life I want for them with a scholarship income."

"You are not going to be on a scholarship forever. Once you complete a Ph.D, you'll have a high-earning job. What exactly are you looking for anyway? You can't reproduce the life you had with exactly the same job you had." I said.

"I want to find a job in oil research, or in refining," he said, pacing the parquet floor.

"But those jobs are in Calgary, not in Toronto," I insisted, my voice a few decibels too high.

"I want to stay in Ontario if I can," Jussef said while sliding his right hand over his balding head.

"You know what? Your umbilical cord is too short. You don't want to go to Alberta because you will be too far away from your family."

His mother's side of the family lived in Montreal, and he wanted to stay as close to them as possible. It was somehow reassuring for him to be near maternal grandparents, uncles, and an aunt who were slightly older than us. I kept thinking of Alberta, with its oil-based economy as the final destination. Job interviews started to trickle in, and he heard a few offers.

"They offered me a job in Moose Jaw," Jussef announced one day.

"Where is that?"

"In the middle of nowhere," he said.

Another offer came from a university in Guelph, ON for a Ph.D. in polymers. I got excited about the possibility of enrolling later in a Ph.D. program as well.

"What happened?" I asked.

"I turned it down," he answered. I rolled my eyes all the way to the back of my head.

"Stop rejecting job and scholarship offers. Your luck is going to run out." We were going into the third month of living on our savings.

In preparation for each job interview, we became a team. I pressed his shirts, cleaned the lint off his suits, and packed his overnight luggage. When he returned home, he gave me the report, and we would start all over again.

Together we sent out over two hundred resumes between our arrival on July 7th and the day of Princess Diana's death in late August. My resumes may as well have ended up in Lake Ontario. I never received a response, but by late August I kept my eyes on the reports from Paris.

"I have news," Jussef said when he arrived home one day. "I found a job!"

"You have a job? That's great! Doing what? Where? How much?" I rejoiced and wanted all the details at once while seasoning a ratatouille on the stove, feeding Saul a banana, and keeping my eye out for roaches in the kitchen.

"It's a process engineer position, a good starting point, but far from what I expected. I got a better job when I finished my undergraduate 15 years ago," he whined.

"Oh, come on, don't be grouchy about it. Let's celebrate!" I said.

"I already did. I bought a car!" he said with a broad smile on his face.

"What?"

"Come downstairs. Let me show you." He grabbed my hand and pulled as I tried to get Saul of the door swing he was jumping from.

"You bought a car? How much was it? How much are the monthly payments?"

"There are no monthly payments. I bought it with cash."

"Are you kidding me? You paid cash? What about the down payment for our first home? How much was it?" My body stored up the disappointment since I was too busy with Saul wriggling from my arms because he wanted to be on the floor.

"Easy, Lisbeth. Let's have a look. You'll love it," he said soothingly.

"A Firefly?" I said after we stepped out of the elevator and onto the driveway. "You bought a Firefly? How much did you pay for it? Where are you going to put the car seat?"

"Six thousand. At minimum, I will have what I had in Venezuela."

"Well, congratulations on your job and your car."

*

ZOË CAME TO VISIT. She needed to attend a conference in Toronto and traveled with her daughter Kathy and the nanny. It was the third time we met up in the 10 years since we'd known each other. She looked radiant with her baby; her bright smile illuminated her face, which was framed by a mid-length, dark wavy mane. Always dressed in practical and comfortable clothes, she moved swiftly and spoke with her fast American accent.

"I love the floors," she said as soon as she stepped into our apartment on Sherobee Road. "What a view! I like it," she said, looking out the balcony beyond the Mississauga Hospital.

"What do you like about it?" I asked.

"First, these are parquet floors. They have character, and with all the light coming from the windows, they look stunning. Then you have the view. What floor is this? Twenty?" She held her baby close to her as she looked out the balcony from the living room door.

"Sixteen. The apartment is infected with roaches," I said.

"You haven't lived in New York, dear," she answered back.

We sat on the floor: the nanny, the babies, Zoë and me. I had prepared a simple cheesecake without toppings and a blended juice, which Zoë loved. The babies were adorable together. Saul ran after the girl's food. Three women chatting and marveling over the children's beauty was an especially ordinary moment I'd never had before. I wished we lived closer to each other.

When we got tired of sitting on the floor, we went downstairs to the green space and laughed at the grey squirrels and at the Canadian news.

"Oh, I know. On the TV at the hotel, they spent like five minutes talking about a fallen tree," she said.

"New York and Venezuela have that in common, the news never bores," I laughed.

"Try to get some rest, Lisbeth," she said as we got ready to say goodbye. "I work fultime, and have help because I need adult time. So do you. You need to rest. You need to meet people and do something fun without the kids." She pointed out that I had complained a lot in the few hours we shared and that I needed to relax and to let things happen when they needed to happen. "You made a big decision to move away and leave everything behind. You needed a lot of courage for that, but now you need to concentrate on what's important."

"I don't know what's important anymore. Everything seems so immediate and urgent."

Saul pointed at a squirrel. "Ardilla," I said as we strolled our way to the parking lot to get Zoë's car.

"Life is important, Lis," she said as she waved goodbye from the window of her rented car. "Just allow yourself to be a gal."

Talk Show

THE WEAK SUMMER heat soon ran out and gave way to a brief windy blur called fall. Coming from the tropics, it all felt like deep freeze. Ramón started his new school and joined an ESL class.

The trees dropped their leaves within a week after Labor Day: one Sunday they turned red, the next Sunday they were naked. Just like that. A brief windy spell and all the beauty and glory of the red maples expired.

The first day I saw snow falling in Canada, we were at the Toronto Zoo with Saul in a stroller and Ramón running around excited, commenting on everything he saw. On our way to the cafeteria for a lunch break, we saw something falling from the sky, and I decided to go out and investigate. I told Jussef, "Watch the kids," and ran outside. I closed my eyes and lifted my face to let the snow touch my cheeks and experience its cold fingertips on my skin. I opened my mouth and tried to catch some with my tongue.

Some passersby asked, "Is this your first time?"

"Yes," I said.

"Wait until you have to shovel it from your driveway," they yelled as they passed.

Soon, Jussef and the kids joined me outside. The beauty of our first snowfall in Toronto mesmerized us all. Thick snowflakes fell, softly dissolving as soon as they hit the ground like oversized white confetti falling in slow motion. A woman stared at us with a big smile on her face.

"Buy the children snowsuits at the thrift store because they outgrow their new clothes before the winter is over," she said.

We bought little Saul a zippered suit with booties and Ramón a snow jacket, which he refused to button on his way to school. "It's too hot," he said.

We soon found out that was not nearly enough.

In September, we got two feet of snow in one night. It blocked the roads and made us doubt our decision to come. We were so ill-prepared for this part of the journey. I had seen snow on the ground a few times before, once in 1990 when I visited Jussef in Cincinnati. But I had never experienced snowfall before. We needed words to name our new reality. The quality of snow involved a long vocabulary list: We used *crisp* and *sparkly* when fresh; *sticky* meant the children could make a snowman, or throw snowballs; *fluffy* was good for skiing, but I wouldn't even try. *Slushy* came with wet showers, or after several days on the ground; best of all was when you walked in the dark and there was a full moon – that we called *shimmering*.

Snow required clothes we didn't even know existed: long johns and thermal underwear that cut libido and made us giggle. Snow pants, snow boots, gloves, hats, and scarves made us look like astronauts. We needed a snow cover for the stroller and sleds for the kids. We spent more money and continued to deplete our savings. Stress accumulated like the snow banks in the parking lots I passed as I made my way to job training and volunteer hours.

We went to Montreal for Thanksgiving. Jussef's family had prepared a welcoming reception for us. The whole clan had been invited. His uncle George and aunt Dahlal hosted the party and welcomed us with big hugs as if we had known each other all our lives. They invited us in, showed us our bedrooms, and all the food they had prepared in celebration. While Ramón talked to their children, Saul tried to play with a parakeet inside a cage over the counter of the great kitchen. I felt welcomed and warm in their house in a way I never felt with Jussef's family back in Caracas. The rest of Jussef's relatives in Montreal were cold to me and indifferent to Ramón at best. I yearned for a mother and a family to take me and Ramón in, but the harder I tried, the more I felt that Ramón and I would only be welcomed by a few exceptional people in the extended family. Beyond the social pleasantries, they referred to Ramón as "your son" and to Saul as "Jussef's baby." I felt they eyed me from above their shoulders, a gesture I came to associate with Jussef's family, both in Caracas and in Montreal.

I welcomed the linguistic diversity of the family. I could hear four languages spoken at any given time: French, English, Arabic and Spanish. Also, I enjoyed the food. Any meal was a feast fit for kings.

"Your English is so good. I didn't expect you to speak English at all," I would hear from time to time.

In January of 1998, it rained ice. It rained ice on frozen tree branches and frozen electric lines. A foot of freezing rain or more fell during the six-day downpour. Millions of Canadian citizens were trapped all the way from Ottawa to Quebec City, from Montreal to Halifax. The trees gave in to the weight and fell on electric lines. Without electricity or heat, plumbing broke and house basements filled with raw sewage. People froze to death inside their houses, while thousands of citizens struggled without electricity in subzero temperatures – some for more than a month. Others packed the overcrowded shelters. In the *Globe and Mail*, East Canada appeared striking and utterly devastated in what was known as the Ice Storm.

The storm didn't reach Toronto, but I was scared and cold most of the time. The light adjustment continued to be an issue. In the summer, I would go non-stop until 11:30 p.m. because I still saw light outside my window. Now, the days were shorter, and I didn't know when I had to go to sleep. I felt spent by 4 p.m..

*

JUSSEF MET CARLOS POSADA, an operator in the lubricant plant and an established immigrant from Guatemala with incredibly beautiful black hair, a silver strand in the middle. He and his wife Ana, a librarian with wide Bette-Davis eyes, had two children: a young man and a teenage girl. Carlos and Ana were a bit older than us. Carlos and Ana invited us to meet their friends, Nacho Lopez and Cecilia Manzanera, from Mexico. Nacho had a sharp sense of humor and made fun of everything all of the time. Cecilia was Zoë but Latina, giving beyond measure, and always with practical advice and money saving tips. Besides, I loved that she went by her maiden name, as I did. We also met with Mary and Jack from Venezuela and Poland, respectively. Mary had been my roommate in Venezuela and had married Jack, an immigrant from Poland. Maxime and Frank, from Zaire, completed our small group of friends and acquaintances. Frank was the first person Jussef met in Canada, when he was still alone and looking for a place to live. When Frank's wife arrived, the men gathered the two families in a park to celebrate our budding friendship.

We also made contact with the growing Venezuelan community, but it was clear to me right away that I didn't belong. When we met with these people, I felt the same way as in the presence of Jussef's family, small and inadequate. One woman visited my apartment and flipped my dishes to see the brand.

I was indiscreet, told sexual jokes, and was coarse and blunt in my way of speaking. I didn't use euphemisms; I called things by their names. At a house party, I noticed two women speaking in hushed voices. One looked at me from head to toe as she told her companion, "La sacó de abajo," as if my husband had lifted me from the ground. I felt there was a hidden between them and my sister-in-law and mother in-law back in Venezuela. The type of conversations they brought up was the first similarity.

"Coiman? Where is that name from? That's not very common," somebody always asked.

"I don't know. It's my grandmother's last name; she was a single mother. She was Black so it's probably one of those names passed on by slave owners." I thought this was an honest answer, but it somehow made people feel uncomfortable.

Coincidences made me uncomfortable. In a phone conversation with my mother in-law, I mentioned that I disliked octopus, but it seemed to be readily available in Canada. Days later, we were invited to a get-together at one Venezuelan family's place. They served pasta with octopus. There had to be a conspiracy with my mother-in-law or my mother. When I talked about this with Jussef, he replied to me that my imagination played tricks on me. That made me angry that he didn't understand my anxiety.

Soon, I started to believe news stories on TV were about me. One about a boy with cropped hair seemed to be an obvious reference to my "bad hair" and my rather masculine manners, I thought. One afternoon, the phone rang.

"Is this Lisbeth Coiman?" a voice asked.

"That's me. Who's speaking?" I frowned, trying to recognize the voice.

"I am calling from a popular TV talk show, and we want you to participate in an episode about immigrants."

I was hesitant and thought back to the news story about the boy with the cropped hair. I worried it was too much of a coincidence. "How did you get my name and number?" I asked.

Alone in the kitchen, I stared at the beige wall, noticing a hole near the telephone line. I felt the small kitchen closing in on me, suffocating me.

"How are you doing in your new home?" the voice asked, not answering my question.

"When they gave us the landed immigrant papers at the embassy, they made us feel valuable, as if Canada needed us. But then people didn't treat us right."

"How's that?" the woman continued asking questions.

I took a deep breath and ranted. "My husband wore out his shoes looking for a place to live, and then he had to put ten months payment in advance because he didn't have references. Then we got this apartment infected with roaches. I don't like where we live, but we were unable to find a better rental. And I can't find a job. I think the postal service throws my resumes and cover letters into the Lake Ontario; honestly, I never hear a response. Now we are struggling, that's how we are doing. It's not easy. We have to prove ourselves even to obtain a driver's license. It is an uphill battle, and we are stressed out."

"Why did you come then?" she said with frustration in her voice.

"Because we hoped for a better future for our children. In Venezuela, education doesn't exist as it does here. I remember trying to enroll my young child in first grade in a public school and the front door was almost blocked with a pile of broken desks. I see the school my son goes to here, clean and bright, full of resources, with professional teachers, who come to school on time and show up for work every day, and think this is what we came here for."

The person on the phone said she would call again. I stared at the hole in the wall.

"Who was this talk show host?" asked Jussef when he came back from work, and I had told him about my day.

"I don't know," I answered. "I don't watch afternoon TV. I don't know about a show hosts."

"Lisbeth, are you sure of this? It sounds fake," he insisted.

"I think it must have been my friend from Venezuela, the radio talk-show host. Remember that show when they interviewed me about immigration? She must've given them my number." A few weeks later, I received two more related phone calls that made me think that I was being monitored or under surveillance.

The first call was from an uncle from Venezuela. He didn't sound interested in me, his niece, but in the political questions he asked in a business tone. I told him that we lived in a neighborhood where most people were refugees. We were struggling, Jussef had a job, but it was an uphill battle, and we were already feeling the impact of the weather. He said, and this is when I felt that he wasn't speaking to me as an uncle but from a political platform of some sort, that Chavez was visiting Canada and asked what I thought about him. Then he asked if the best I could do with what I took from my country was to live in a refugee neighborhood.

"I didn't take anything from Venezuela. We brought our degrees and our suitcases and a few boxes with books," I said and hung up, realizing he had done a political survey on me. The hole in the wall was now clearly a camera that I tried to ignore.

Gabi, a neighbor from the apartment on Avenida Andrés Bello, contacted me to say she had listened to me on the radio.

"Yes, they are still airing that interview," I said, dismissing her.

"No, Lisbeth, this is another conversation. You were talking about Canada," Gabi insisted.

"It must've been my uncle who broadcast our conversation."

From my corner in the kitchen, I watched Saul play with a second-hand toy bought at a garage sale on the parquet floor, light streaming from the large living room windows.

"All is good," I told myself.

The second time the mysterious talk show host called, I was concerned with the way I looked in front of the camera hidden in my kitchen. I refused her invitation to her show. It felt real.

"We can send a limo," she insisted.

"No, I don't want to," I replied, irritated. "You can use my story, but I won't go anywhere."

"Thank you for your time," she said abruptly and hung up. I looked into the hole in the wall and bawled.

"I need help," I yelled to the hole.

*

WE HAD BEEN in Canada for fewer than ten months. To land a decent job reference, I volunteered, teaching English as a Second Language to new immigrants, and sorted donated clothes for the Intercultural Neighborhood Community Social Services. The agency matched newcomers to volunteer hosts, who showed us around and helped us establish a support network. Although I was aiming for a job, I had to pay for babysitting to volunteer.

At the front desk one day, I ran into a man from Venezuela I had met briefly in the Canadian Embassy in Caracas. We acknowledged each other at the reception. Then, I continued inside while he sat to wait for his turn to get an interview for the Newcomer Program. I didn't see him leave.

The agency gave me a long list of contact numbers of newcomers to call. Program alumni. I called them from my home, asked them for feedback, took notes, and returned their files to the office. The Venezuelan man I had run into was on that list. Another coincidence. He was under the impression that I had jeopardized his chances for an interview. He thought I was guilty of the rejection he received. I volunteered tirelessly to get a reference, and he thought I had the power to limit his chances. Preposterous. Or maybe not. Maybe I had a magical influence on his case. Maybe they all watched me because I was this special woman that Venezuelans wanted back, and they were all trying to make me see my mistake of immigrating to Canada.

For the first time, I noticed my stuttering and speech problems. I don't remember if I spoke Spanish or English, but my mouth wouldn't make the correct sounds. I kept confusing words and mispronouncing them. I caught all the mistakes, but was speaking too fast to correct them.

Breaking Point

ZOË AND I CORRESPONDED daily via email. I enjoyed these immediate exchanges with fascination. We told each other what our babies were doing. She told me about her struggle to find a reliable babysitter. The one she trusted since her daughter's birth was moving onto something else. Zoë was also looking for a guy, a partner, a male person to complete the family she envisioned for her daughter. We called frequently, usually to clarify things, or check if something had arrived. We still used snail mail to send cards and pictures, but most of our exchanges occurred over email.

Her optimistic letters cheered me up, and I enjoyed the ordinary details of a mother interacting with her baby. She always dropped a line to encourage me to live a more positive life.

> The baby runs all over the place, opens the drawers and plays with everything she finds. She is learning "nose," "eyes," "mouth," pointing with her finger at herself or at others. She says "nana" for banana. Sometimes she gives you a whole sentence of gibberish. This is the best experience of my life.
>
> Try to have some rest, Lisbeth. You are stressed out, and need to have a break. You haven't stopped once since you got

landed immigrant status. Everybody needs to rest, even such a strong woman like you.

Love

Zoë

*

AT 18-MONTHS-OLD, Saul laughed as he emptied cabinets and flushed small objects down the toilet. He climbed on the boxes we had packed in preparation for our move to Meadowvale. We canvased all of Mississauga's districts looking for a suitable place for our small family and even explored the possibility of purchasing a house. We decided to move as soon as Ramón completed seventh grade, only a few weeks away.

"Do you hit Saul? Are you mean to him when I am not looking?" I asked Ramón one day without any evidence.

"Why are you even asking me that?"

"Jamil said in Venezuela that you could do that," I answered.

"And you decided to believe him." My wise 12 year-old squinted at me and shook his head.

We were no longer comrades—those children who had gone through difficult times and had learned to ride bikes and play baseball together were gone. I had become the aggressor. I scolded him for not doing his chores and for not helping with childcare. I accused him of bullying Saul.

"I am sorry, Ramón. I am so sorry." I wanted his forgiveness right there, but something delicate and precious had broken.

Despite recognizing that I had been wrong, I continued harassing my son at home, yelling at him for minor mistakes, for not doing his homework, for being a boy.

At school, Ramón wasn't having a good time either. As a newcomer, he hadn't found a group to stick with and was an easy prey for bullies. Soon, he got into a fight with a taller student, who quickly overpowered him. To avoid more blows from his opponent, he played possum until a teacher came to find out why he was lying on the ground. The teachers were not amused, but I thought he was wonderful. I took him to a doctor to see if anything was broken. The doctor recommended he join karate classes.

I insisted and Jussef agreed with me on pulling Ramón out of the school and advance the date of our move by two weeks. I didn't see any relation between my son's new problems at school and my own now bizarre behavior. The day we moved from Cooksville to Meadowvale, there was a severe thunderstorm watch, and the helpers we hired didn't show up. It was part of the conspiracy to ridicule me and make my life more difficult than it ought to be.

The new apartment on Battleford Road was located in a rental complex near Lake Aquitaine, where people caught and released fish in the summer and played ice hockey in the winter. Urban trails connected the neighborhoods with a small shopping mall, a community center, bus stops, and schools. A few daffodils poked out of the snow to greet the neighbors. Three weeks later, we heard the distinct noise of lawnmowers and weed-eaters, the official signal for spring. Despite the warming temperatures, I didn't want to leave the apartment.

"Hurry, up. We are going to miss the fireworks," said Jussef. The family wanted to enjoy the Victoria Day festivities.

"Todavía está muy frío. I don't want to sit on the ground," I protested.

"Mamá vamos. Aren't you tired of being inside?" Ramón asked while I got Saul ready to celebrate Victoria Day.

Our apartment was on the ground floor, had two bedrooms, one and half bathrooms, a living/dining room, a small kitchen, and a porch. We kept the blinds down all the time. Although the apartment had plenty of windows, it felt a little cavernous. Four cypresses separated the porch from the parking lot, which made the place look even darker. Unpacked boxes lay everywhere.

Even though I worried that my anxious behavior might be affecting my son, I kept the focus on myself amid the chaos of moving boxes. In a letter to Zoë, I expressed to her my concern about being ridiculed in public.

> They say these are record-breaking temperatures, that there hasn't been a summer this hot in years. It is hot, but it's the humidity that bothers me. It's sticky.
> Saul made a little friend at Ramón's baseball practice, an adorable red-haired toddler. It's fun to see them playing together, but I can't help feeling uncomfortable while sitting on the bleachers. I feel everybody is making fun of me. They think I'm a transgender man and they poke fun at that, because of that thing on my face.

Between opening boxes and taking care of Saul, I didn't have time to read Zoë's response, in which she asked me to call her back immediately.

I put Saul in his crib for an afternoon nap while Ramón watched the World Cup on TV. I started dinner, trying to keep a routine during the longer days of our second summer in Canada. The phone rang.

"What's going on?" It was Zoë, full of questions and an unfamiliar urgency. "I read your email last night. I asked you to call me. Tell me what's up. What's this about people making fun of you during Ramón's baseball practice? I don't get it."

"I don't know how to explain this, Zoë. There is this guy at the baseball practice. He is a parent. He thinks I am some sort transgender or transvestite."

"Wait, wait, wait," she interrupted. "Who thinks that?"

"Everybody. They're talking about me."

"How do you know that?"

"Well, I overheard the guy at the baseball practice telling this good news/bad news joke to another person. He said, 'Good news, we have a new baseball player from Venezuela. Bad news that's the mother,' and then he pointed his chin at me."

"Did you really hear that? See that?" She peppered me with questions.

"Yeah. Then the guy made some gestures as if I was a gay man or something. I wouldn't care if I was a lesbian, but I'm not. They think I'm a deviant. You know, that thing on my face, sometimes people wonder what the heck it is, but this guy was so obvious."

"Somebody must be feeling awfully bad about himself to initiate rumors like that. Where's that baseball practice, Lisbeth? Is that in your new neighborhood?"

"No. It's where we lived before by Sherobee Road. I registered Ramón in baseball before we moved to Meadowvale, and now I have to drive all the way south for practice. It's a long drive. My mother is also telling everybody that I was born a boy and that they chopped it off."

"They chopped what off?"

"My penis."

"Why would she say that about her daughter?"

"Because I want to play baseball. All my brothers play baseball, but they only allow me to be the queen. I don't want to be a queen. I want to play baseball." I sobbed quietly.

"How old are you, Lisbeth?"

"34. Why?"

"Oh, I see. That happened when you were a little girl? Right now, I say take him out of the baseball practice because you already have a gazillion things on your platter. You are still walking around unpacked boxes, getting to know your neighborhood, finding the library, the nearest park. Those things are more important right now. You have a toddler and a teenager, and you are a recent immigrant. You've moved twice. I really suggest no baseball."

"Oh, Zoë. I mean summer days drag forever; he is twelve going on thirteen. It's difficult to keep him busy, especially with the baby and all."

"Lisbeth, you're too stressed out. You've moved twice in ten months. You moved from your home country, for God's sake, less than a year ago. You need to take a break. I say, just take the boys to the pool and hang out. Do nothing."

"I think Ramón's hurting Saul."

"What?"

I wiped my runny nose and the tears off my face with my sleeve.

"Ok. Lisbeth, let's stop here for a sec'. What gave you that idea?"

"A few days before leaving Venezuela, Jussef's younger brother called. He said he was worried that Ramón would hurt Saul because they were only half brothers. Now I'm worried sick about it."

"It doesn't surprise me considering who it came from. You're smart and should be able to laugh at the absurdity of that statement. If you can't put it down, it's because it bothers you somewhere deep." Her next question hit the target. "Were you ever molested or raped?"

"BRRRR. BRRRR. BRRRR." A thin line of urine ran down my leg.

"That's not an answer."

"Yes and no."

"Why no?"

"Because I never said 'no.' It was my fault."

"Why yes?" Her words got under my skin.

"He is my brother." I yelled into the phone. "I don't want to talk about that now or ever! It happened. OK? There is nothing I can do to erase that. What good will it do to talk about it?"

I was yelling and sobbing. Snot rushed over my lips. I held the phone between my neck and shoulder and wiped my face with my shirt as she spoke softly on the phone.

"I just wanna help. One day you'll have to talk about it, sooner rather than later. From what I am hearing, that crap is coming out the wrong way. You're putting your ugly memories on your son, your wonderful son. If you're not careful, you're going to hurt him the same way that witch hurt you. You hear me? What else is going on?"

"Oh, Zoë. This conversation is going to cost you too much money."

"I have a good phone plan and locking you up is going to be much more expensive. Start speaking, hon, I'm listening."

"There are cameras all over."

"Where?"

"Here, in the apartment. They're looking at me from inside the TV. There are speakers hidden in the fireplace, cameras in the bookshelves, and a tape recorder in a hole in the kitchen wall. They want to know all I do and say and then they show that on TV and radio, in Venezuela and around the world in the big screens of the World Cup stadiums. They also have chat rooms on the Internet, and they talk about me. People are watching me all over the world. They're laughing at me. I'm a joke. The only safe place is my walk-in closet. They even watch when I'm having sex."

"Smile. You're on Candid Camera, honey," She made a joke, and I chuckled. She said that was good that I was able to get a joke. Then she continued asking questions. "Who are *they*?"

"There are two teams. There's a team led by my mother. There's another team led by you. One's a bad team; the other's a good team."

"Am I in the good team?"

"Yes. You're the leader of the good team."

"I'm glad to hear that, Lisbeth," she said, her voice breaking. "And I am sorry your mom hurt you so badly. What are we competing about?"

"Mom wants to prove I'm evil because I don't love her."

"Did you tell her you don't love her? You should. One of these days when she calls to tell you she's going to show up at your door, tell her, 'I don't want you here. I don't love you.' She needs to hear that."

"No, I never told her. Somebody asked why we left Venezuela, and I said because I couldn't stand being near my mother or my mother-in-law anymore. Somebody told them, and now my mother wants to prove I'm evil."

"You are not evil."

"I think I am. I have done bad things. I had sex with my brother. I have an ugly face, and I can't make anybody love me. I'm a fucking loser. I can't get a job. My in-laws think I am a social climber. I'm a joke."

"You don't need a job right now. I mean, you could use the money. But your job now is to settle your family in your new country. That's a great responsibility, and you won't be able to do that if you break down. You have to stay put. What else is going on?"

"I'm remembering a lot. I always remembered my childhood, but I somehow managed to put it away. Now I can't. It's like watching myself in a mirror, but the mirror is in pieces. Every part of me – every event of my childhood – is reflected in this new place. Your team is making me remember."

"My team? How come?"

"Your team wants to show my childhood. Everything is on TV and radio and the internet. Too many things are similar."

"Like what?"

"There was this show. A young Venezuelan couple made a presentation about our political situation. They said that Venezuela is a wonderful country with many tourist attractions, then they spoke ill about what's happening right now."

"Somebody you met?"

"No. On TV. They spoke and showed images, videos, of beautiful places like landmarks. One of the places they showed was Salto La Llovizna. It's a national park in the souteast of the country. There's a waterfall with a thick mist. I saw this, and I remembered there was a tragedy there when I was a little girl. A group of teachers went there for a workshop or something. When they were crossing the hanging bridge over the falls, the bridge gave way and the teachers died. Suddenly, it was as if I were five years old again, crying because the teachers were dead. I think it's a hidden message for me."

"What's the message?"

"I'm a teacher now. I should avoid bodies of water. That's why I don't want to take the children to the swimming pool."

"Ok. What else is similar?"

"I can hear my brothers' and my mother's voices coming out of the speakers in the fireplace. They taunt me. They are always making fun of me. The other day I was watching the World Cup on TV, and I could read the names my siblings called me on the back of the uniforms of the entire Romanian team. The team was lined up to sing their national anthem, and on the back of their shirts I read *Bembona*, *Pata e' Lancha*, *Esquiadora*, *Chismosa.* I started crying and turned off the TV and Ramón got angry because he wanted to watch the game. I fought him. It wasn't good."

"Did you hit him?"

"No, but I was close. Jussef came to defend Ramón. Jussef always stands up for him like his own blood. Everybody's asking me these weird questions too, as if they already know about me before we meet. The questions are in a book that is getting passed around. Everybody has read the questions. Even you."

"Me? Yeah, Lisbeth, I read the book, and my favorite character is your mother," she said with irony. "Tell me what else is similar?"

"The rain is not real."

"How come?"

"There are film crews making rain happen right here in front of my apartment."

"Why?"

"They want me to remember the rain."

"Why?"

"Cockroaches. Before the rain, the cockroaches come out. They are monsters, and they fly. I ate one. I can't eat anything now; it's still in my mouth. She gets really angry because I don't want to eat food. She pulls my hair back, and when I yell with my mouth open, she shoves the spoon inside my mouth and down my throat."

"Who is force-feeding you?" asked Zoë.

"My mom."

"What happens then?"

"She tells me that if I throw up I will have to eat it. She screams at me all the time from the hole in the kitchen wall. She says, 'Carolina this, Carolina that.' I hate that name."

"Wait, who's Carolina?"

"That's my middle name. They all call me Carolina. But I hate it. She also calls me "maldita muchacha. muchacha 'el demonio." She says that the devil will visit me at night and pull my feet while I sleep."

"Is she religious?"

"No, she isn't. But she surely talks about the devil all the time and likes horror movies. The thing is, I can't sleep. I keep thinking that something really bad is going to happen if I fall asleep, like the devil's going to enter my room like she always told me. Am I evil?"

"Oh, dear Lis, you aren't evil. You're just somebody hurting really bad."

I sobbed uncontrollably. We had been on the phone for nearly an hour. I felt that Zoë would hang up soon—to go to an appointment or just to get off the line.

"Where's Saul?" she asked changing the subject.

"I don't know."

"Turn around, please" she said softly. "Tell me, where is Ramón? Call Ramón."

"Ramón," I called.

"¿Qué?"

"Nada, sólo quiero saber dónde estás."

"Mom, I am right here. Can't you see me?" he said, rolling his eyes upward, impatient, as any teenager with the absurdity of his family life. He was sitting right in front of the TV, a mere eight feet away from the kitchen's threshold where I stood with the phone to my ear.

"He is here. Watching TV."

"That's fine." She continued with the same softness. "Ask Ramón to find Saul?"

"¿Ramón, puedes ver qué está haciendo Saul?" Ramón got up from the couch and walked the few steps to the bedroom.

From the bedroom, he reported back, "Saul is here. He is sleeping."

"Lis, I'm going to have to hang up soon. Before we do that, please give me Jussef's phone number at work. I think I need to talk to him."

"You never wanted to talk to Jussef before." I hesitated. "Why do you want to talk to him now?"

"You're very sick, Lisbeth."

"How?"

"You're psychotic. Do you know what that means, honey?"

"No, but I think it's bad. Am I crazy?"

She didn't say yes or no. "You need immediate medical attention. I don't know anybody who has suffered so much as a child, and I don't understand why people do this to their children, but you are safe now. You will receive help, but you need to trust Jussef and me. Will you? I need to hear that you trust us."

"I will trust you, but I can't trust Jussef anymore."

"You've got to trust him. We don't have any other option. You're alone in Mississauga, in Canada. You have two children. I'm the only other person around, and I'm in Manhattan. You've gotta trust Jussef."

I gave her the phone number. "Tell Ramón to get ready to go to summer camp." Zoë said.

"How's he going to get there?"

"Team Zoë will take him there. Don't worry. Now, what I want you to do is take a chair from the kitchen, put it out on the porch and do nothing for a half hour. Can you do that for me? Just enjoy that Saul is sleeping and Ramón is watching TV."

"I can't do that; I have to cook dinner. My mother and my mother-in-law are watching me on TV, and they will know I am not doing my chores."

"You'll have hot dogs for dinner tonight. Listen carefully. I love you, Lisbeth; Jussef loves you; Ramón loves you; Saul loves you. There are four people here who love you and need you. Hang on to that love and stay put. I will call you tomorrow."

I put the receiver back and went to the bathroom to wash my face. I blew my nose, and pulled my hair in a ponytail. I checked on Saul sleeping in his crib, watched his chest expand with his breath, and noticed his small hand next to his rosy cheeks. I passed by Ramón still watching TV, and dragged a chair to the porch. I sat down, focusing on the ants crawling on Saul's toy truck on the ground, the cypresses shielding me from the camera crews outside.

*

ZOË CALLED EVERY DAY for the next month. She put aside her dislike for Jussef to coach him. In the process, they became friends, and her influence caused some changes on how he took control of our chaotic home.

Whatever it was that guided her through those conversations happened just in time. I had yet to visit the darkest place of madness. The memories of the days and weeks that followed are all unreliable to me. I can only partially remember what happened and count heavily on Jussef to tell this part of the story.

Within a week, Ramón was safe at a summer camp in Maine. We never knew how much it cost. Zoë made the arrangements, paid for transportation and tuition for a month, and even gave him pocket money. Saul was only 18 months old and spent several hours a day safe in day care.

Shattered Mirror

I ARGUED FREQUENTLY with Jussef, and it was getting ugly. During one argument, a cup flew out of my hands and crashed into a mirror we had just bought at a garage sale.

"Are you crazy? Ahora vamos a tener mala suerte," said Jussef worried that the shattered mirror could bring us bad luck.

There had been two main pieces to my breakdown. First was paranoia manifesting in the fear of being chased, spied upon, monitored, or exposed as a petty criminal and a fraud. Second was the uncontrolled flow of painful images reemerging from my childhood, the faces and the events floating around in front of me:

> *My blonde-bleached mother beating us with a three-inch leather belt soaked in salt water; my brother wrestling me to the ground, our pants going off, his penis inside me; another brother burning my doll house and destroying my ocean cards collection; an earthquake rattling Caracas when I was three or four, boulders falling down onto the road and my father veering the car out of danger, and my mother murmuring avemarías; cockroaches coming out before the rain; my parents fighting; the horror films, my brothers scaring me in the middle of the night; meona, chicharronua; the bullying.*

Years later, as I tried to remember the days of my breakdown, I asked Jussef what happened after I talked to Zoë and before he decided to take me to the hospital. He told me what he remembered, which wasn't much.

"The day after Zoë called me, I registered Saul in YMCA," he says.

To convince him to come along, Jussef told little Saul they would stop at the tracks and he would be able to touch the rails. Every morning, on their way to the daycare, Jussef had to stop at the rail track, open the door, get Saul out and let him touch the rails. It was his thing, and he beamed after doing that. "The rest was easy," Jussef said. The baby loved the daycare right away.

Jussef left Saul at the YMCA in the mornings and picked him up in the afternoons. "Once I came back home to find you inside the walk-in closet. You were crying and talking like a little girl."

"What did I say?" I asked.

'I don't want to do that. I don't want to do that.' You said it over and over again in a girl's voice. You rocked back and forth, sitting on the carpet inside the closet with your knees to your chest, and your arms wrapped around your legs. You howled, too. It was scary."

"I'm sorry. What did you do?" I asked.

"I tried to get you out of the closet, tell you that Saul and Ramón were here, that you needed to take care of your sons. I asked you if you knew you had two sons." He stopped talking then, and we hugged in silence.

Asking his family for help had been out of the question. That much I knew. They had never approved of our relationship to begin with. An uncle and his wife from Boston came to Toronto for a conference and took a short detour to visit us in Mississauga. Jussef didn't want his family to know that anything was wrong. I learned to pass for sane.

"We just felt that you were under enormous stress, but we couldn't tell you were having a breakdown. We would have helped," his aunt told me years later.

The calls from Venezuela kept me anchored in time and place, even though I wanted to leave so desperately. I don't remember if my sister called me or if I called her, but she became a messenger.

"Mom wants to know what it is that you have against her," she said one time.

"Tita," I said, "I just don't want mom around me. She keeps telling me over the phone she will show up at our door. I don't want that to happen."

My sister interrupted. "Why?"

"It's difficult to explain over the phone. It has to do with the things she told the boys when I got angry as a child. She told them to put a finger inside of me because I was hysterical, and one of them did, more than a finger. I can't talk about these things on the phone with her. It'll kill her."

"It will. She said that, but she didn't mean that," Tita explained.

"Well I think that's an awful thing to say to one's daughter." I raised my eyes to the ceiling and noticed the red light of the smoke alarm alerting me of the cameras hiding in the apartment.

"I grew up in the same home, and I'm not traumatized by that. It wasn't that bad." She challenged me as if I had not just revealed a piece of dreadful experience to her.

I pulled myself together, the best I could, and said, "I'm glad you love your mother so much, but your mother and my mother are two different people. I don't love her, I don't want her by my side, and I'm not in the financial condition of receiving visitors from abroad." I hung up.

Jussef then called my older brother and told him that something was wrong with me, but he couldn't get any help from my brother except the commitment for the family to avoid sharing problems with me when we talked over the phone. It was better if the family didn't call at all.

I listened to Jussef speaking on the phone while I sat in front of the TV, pulling out my hair in chunks.

*

BY THEN, JUSSEF was overwhelmed. The pressure of my problems and the prospect of hospitalization and two children without family support was a lot to take in. He told Zoë he felt he was losing me, that I wasn't the same person. He said that I behaved like a child. She reassured him that as soon as I found help I would go back to my old self. She advised him to give me a reliable structure, to come back from work always at the same time. She also suggested demanding that Ramón stick to a routine when he came back from camp. Zoë became so invested in our drama that we hardly made a step forward without consulting her. That wasn't good either, but we didn't have anybody else.

"I felt the same as when my father was dying. I felt you were dying, what I knew and loved of you was dying," Jussef told me when he remembered my breakdown years later.

On Canada Day, a year after our arrival, Jussef took us to the Mississauga Civic Center. In a print summer dress with bright green leaves on a black background, and a wide rim lemon hat, I walked by kiosks trying foods and smiling broadly at people. The dress kept sliding off, so I put Saul's little backpack on my right shoulder to hold the fabric in place. The clothes I had brought from Venezuela hung loose on me.

I could only feel bits of images at a time: folk music, a sentence by a storyteller, children laughing and clapping, the Canadian flag, hot dogs, the smell of curry and fried plantains, black people wearing colorful turbans. It was a well-organized cheerful festivity celebrating my arrival to Canada.

People are not supposed to point at me; they know it distresses me. They are not supposed to make me feel singled out, but I know it is all for me, and I am so grateful. Zoë's team is splendid. I feel like a queen.

When we tired of walking, we sat on the ground near the car show. I looked at an old model, with my head tilted to one side and thought, *they repaired my father's car so well, but they painted it orange. It used to be pink.* I tried to keep little Saul by my side while Jussef snapped pictures.

I lifted my eyes and admired the urban environment of tall, modern buildings, surrounded by an anonymous crowd and Canadian flags.

> *Multitude of people have come to see me, the brown woman with the funny face. Canada Day is just the excuse they use to gather the crowd. From the chat rooms on the internet and from email messages, the news has spread that I, the mysterious woman everybody was talking about, is in town and that this is the opportunity to make me feel welcome.*

Back in the apartment, I went to the bathroom. I looked at myself in the mirror, but the mirror was shattered. In the reflections my thick lips floated away. My round behind reflected in a jagged piece of glass. I reached out to touch the pieces, but then they disappeared. An image of my small breasts extending with the pressure of milk, drops of blood coming out from the nipples staining my brilliant college papers appeared and disappeared too. My mediocre undergraduate thesis floated between fragments of my big feet and my scarred face. A close-up to the chin showed a three-day old unshaven beard. I tried again to touch the shattered mirror, but it kept eluding me, beyond reach, beyond repair, beyond redemption. I saw a Medusa head in front of me. My eyes the color of cockroaches, wide open and dark.

I screamed to the mirror calling myself bitch.

I ran out of the bathroom to the computer and deleted everything on the desktop. All the emails to and from Zoë were gone with a click of the mouse.

*

JUSSEF TOOK SAUL and me for a walk in the park. Jussef held my hand as we strolled along a path surrounded by tall maples and firs. A family party went on in a kiosk in the park. Music reached us, and Jussef invited me to dance. My dress spun in a circle. My mind continued without me. Red gingham jumper. One lost button can't hold the shoulder strap. The front lops to one side, while the white blouse peaks out from the waist, like the tongue of a thirsty dog; white socks rolled over dirty black shoes. Stains of mud and dirt on my jumper. Mess of frizzy caramel curls. I skip behind my four brothers, all in khaki pants, black shoes and white shirts. We look unkempt and wild. We have been in a fight, all of us. Mother waits for us at the door. We enter one by one; I am the last. She slaps the back of my head and says, "Yellow dyke. Bachaca, machorra."

There was no coherence anymore, just flashes of memories flooding my mind. With every image, I tried to make sense of the meaning, thus eliciting a complicated chain of associations, always looking for logic. My thoughts sped so fast I couldn't keep up with them and got lost.

"People are smiling at us, Jussef; some are pointing."

"Lis, you are dancing. That's why people are looking. It's OK to dance in a park on a summer day; don't worry. Let them look."

I burst out crying, and Jussef herded Saul and me into the car. We rushed home.

I locked myself in the dark, cool walk-in closet. Sitting on the carpet, hugging my knees to my chest, I bawled. The smell of open sewage and festering innards altogether make me dizzy. Nausea and repulsion possess me; my head is spinning, and I can see that I will not hold much longer. She flies onto me. Terror knots in my throat. I shake my body with all the strength I can summon, and slam her against the ground. She falls on her back. I see her moving in desperate attempts to turn herself around and continue fighting.

"Are you in the closet again?" asked Jussef. "Look at you, honey, you are a mess. Ah, mi amor, don't cry anymore. Everything is going to be ok." He found me sitting in a corner of the walk-in closet, head down, my knees up to my chest, my hair a frizzy mess.

"I gotta write some shit," I said, looking at him with wide eyes.

"You gotta write some shit, and you gotta see a doctor, right now."

"Why? You don't think I can write? Do you think you are the only intelligent person in the room? Do you think I can only cook for you and take care of your children?"

"No, Lisbeth. Don't try to pick a fight with me. I think you can write all right, and that you are a very smart woman. I wouldn't have fallen for you if you weren't. Now that you are lucid, let me show you what you are writing." He grabbed my hand and guided me to the bathroom. "You see this Ikea box in the bathroom? Do you see the kitchen wall? Do you see these papers?"

The bathroom cabinets were filled with scribbles of short incoherent phrases. There were lists of names and places on the kitchen wall written in pencil, almost illegible. Jussef showed me a stack of pages he'd been collecting, all covered in doodles: geometric shapes and page after page of diagonal grids; curly lines with sprouting leaves; little houses with windows and mountains in the back; flowers, names, and numbers; fragments of writing, like "at 12 being a girl was not good." I wrote lists of all the teachers I had from first grade to college; lists of places I might have visited or not.

"Let's go to the doctor," he said.

Thankfully, we didn't have to worry about the boys. Ramón was in camp and Saul was safely in the care of friends.

False Cognates

AT THE CREDIT VALLEY Hospital, they moved me from the ER into a break room. I sat at a long table, a bright light right over my head. Next to me: a sink and the vending machine. People in hospital scrubs with badges hanging on their chests came in and out of the room to get coffee or drinks from the vending machine and ignored me. I kept crying and rocking back and forth.

A nurse came in, gave me a pop, and left again. Sometime later, I became concerned with the cameras hidden in the bright lamp hanging over the table. I drank a little bit of the pop, but then decided against it. *They are trying to poison me.* I kept rocking and crying.

A tall man talked to me. He introduced himself as the mental health physician on call that night.

"Tell me what's going on," he said as he pulled up a chair.

I felt a high-pressure faucet opening in my heart. I was incoherent, but trying to explain. I talked fast and apparently didn't make any sense.

"Was your country in a war?"

"No," I said indignantly. "These things happened to me as a child. Are you even paying attention to me?"

"You said there were too many casualties." He frowned.

"Yes, there are too many casualties. If I say something here in my house, my mother knows about it when I talk to her on the phone. If I say something to my mother-in-law on the phone, people I am acquainted with here know about it the next day. They are always checking my bags at the stores. People make fun of me, they think I am a transvestite because I have this thing on my face, and I look like a man. And I can't stop remembering my childhood. I want to get out of here. Get me out of here," I yelled.

"Where are you, Lisbeth?" he asked.

"You know where I am! In an interrogation room!" I yelled.

"You are in a hospital, Lisbeth," the doctor said. His voice was calm and reassuring. He kept sipping from his own drink and jotting down notes as he talked to me.

"I am in a state of madness. That's where I am. I thought crazy people were happy, but this is hell. Get me out of here."

"We'll help you. I see you drank the pop. You need to eat and drink lots of fluid. You are dehydrated. We'll give you something to help with that. I'll also prescribe some medicine. You need to make an appointment with your family doctor tomorrow. The doctor will then write a referral to a psychiatrist," he said.

"Are you going to keep me here?" I wanted to know.

"No. We already talked to your husband about it. He is going to take care of you at home. Hang in there. Take your medication as directed." He handed me a pink paper, shook my hand and left. At the bottom of the paper, he had written PTSD and underlined it. I had always wondered about those four words: Post Traumatic Stress Disorder. *Wasn't I in a paranoid delirium?*

False cognates. When I went to Canada, I had been speaking English for over a decade, but it was never natural. I learned English in college. I neither used idioms or cuss words naturally in English, nor any other nuances of the language that required a more in depth linguistic experience. When I dissociated, Spanish took front stage in my communication. Even when speaking in English, I used a lot of cognates. Cognates are identical words in both languages (chocolate, basic, hospital). Although the same word may exist in both languages, it may mean different things. *Actual*, for instance, means in reality in English. *Actual*, in Spanish means current.

In my triage interview with that mental health physician at the Credit Valley Hospital I used the word "casualties" –count of the dead in English. I meant to say too many *casualidades*, which means coincidences. In my mind, my mother, my mother-in-law, the Venezuelans we had met, and the mass media all conspired against me. I suffered a paranoid delirium of an international conspiracy. Everybody was out to get me.

Within an hour, I decided Canada was great. Store clerks could have a blast searching my bags if they enjoyed doing so. I was determined to be happy there, in a place without mothers, mothers-in-law, without cockroaches. I calmed down, and Jussef and I went home. That night, we had the most extraordinary sex we'd in months. I was excited by the presence of film cameras inside our bedroom. "Smile, you're on Candid Camera," I told Jussef. He didn't get the joke.

"What did you tell the doctor at the hospital? I thought he was going to lock me up," I told Jussef while resting in bed after sex. I looked at a tiny dot of green light in the ceiling, the camera light.

"They are worried about Saul," Jussef told me. "They wanted to know if he was in danger. I didn't think so. You fed him and kept him clean. You took him to activities in the community center and read to him frequently. Although you are crazy as a loon, you are a very good mother. He seems happy. That's why they let you go. They wouldn't have let you go if you were suicidal, or if Saul were in danger."

"Ramón is in danger," I said. "Zoë knows it. That's why she sent him to summer camp."

"She didn't say that. She just said it wasn't the best environment for him."

*

WE THOUGHT IT was the end of my issues, but it was just the beginning of a long unmarked path. Dr. Sheldon Silver, a family doctor in the Meadowvale Town Center, became the psychiatrist *de facto* while we waited for the appearance of a mental health professional. A white man in his forties, Dr. Silver commented from time to time about his camping trips or about horses.

The visits to Dr. Silver caused me extreme anxiety. Mothers sat in the waiting room with their babies. The cute, mostly white, blonde and blue-eyed newborns scared me. A fear of displacement got inside me every time I visited that office. I cried my eyes dry in the waiting room sitting among new mothers and senior citizens. It wasn't until many years later that I remembered my mother wanted to replace me with my much fairer newborn brother.

"Your timing couldn't be worse. In summer, all the psychiatrists are playing golf," said Dr. Silver in the examination room of his clinic.

"What am I supposed to do now?"

"A psychiatric nurse will visit you a couple of times a week to check on your medication. It's the best I can do at the moment, given that it's the beginning of summer. Just call my office if you need anything." Dr. Silver didn't sound assuring, but he was all we had during those dark months.

Zoë was livid. She couldn't believe the Canadian medical system would fail her friend in the middle of a psychiatric crisis. She called Dr. Silver many times, and at one point she yelled at him on the phone. Next time I saw him, he made sure to refer to Zoë as Dr. Graves. "Dr. Graves says I'm inept," he said. I was embarrassed because I knew he was trying hard to provide good care for me. Through Dr. Silver we learned something about Zoë.

"What did you tell Dr. Silver? It's funny. He's calling you Dr. Graves," I said on the phone.

"I have a Ph.D. in Psychology."

"But you never told me that."

"It is not relevant. The only thing it's useful for is to put three letters next to my name on a business card when I need to sound official."

"If I had a Ph.D., I'd make sure people knew. I would be so proud. I always say my education will never be complete until I take a Ph.D."

"I am glad you can think about the future, but you have to focus on recovery."

Zoë's credentials came in handy. I had never seen her at work, but she was professional in those conversations with me. She showed empathy and concern but remained steady.

*

THE PROBLEMS IN my new home multiplied. The original medication that the emergency doctor had prescribed sent me into frenzy, and I couldn't sleep for days. I became aggressive against myself. Alone inside the closet, I punched my legs and head, and pulled my hair. If Jussef was home, he tried to calm me down.

"Shush, shush," he'd say and hugged me tenderly as though calming a crying child. Jealousy invaded my thoughts. In my paranoid delirium, Jussef was having sex with everyone but me. In one of my rare lucid moments, I told him I was becoming my mother. All her personality traits were there: aggression, jealousy, and coarse language.

I threw fits against Jussef at the drop of a hat and became more and more difficult to manage. The nurse suggested I visit a crisis center for raped women, which was housed at the Salvation Army building in Mississauga.

"I wasn't raped," I protested.

"But you were severely traumatized. And while we wait for a psychiatrist, you need to talk to somebody who can help you," the nurse told me.

I tried to busy my mind by reading Canadian writers. I had become a fan of Margaret Atwood during college. Alice Munro and Carol Oates also interested me, and I read their work avidly. At the time I went to the Salvation Army, I was reading *Cat's Eye*, and I was sure Atwood had written that book about me.

As I drove to one of my appointments at the crisis center, I became aware of a telecommunication truck behind my car. It was probably the cable company, but the word "telecommunication" sparked psychotic thoughts. They were chasing me. I sped away in the car and inadvertently drove past a red light. When I realized what I had done, I stopped in the middle of the intersection. Saul was in the back seat.

"I shouldn't be driving," was my first statement to the counselor at the center.

After Zoë told me I was psychotic, I never had to wait for anybody to tell me that I was doing something crazy or irrational. As soon as I realized I had done something wrong, I told whoever needed to know so that they made sure I received the help I needed, and they took measures to prevent harm to my sons.

This "psychiatrist-less" situation went on for too long, and Jussef and I called people we knew in mental health careers. I contacted my Psychology professor from college, Marianela Manzanares, a petite woman with an extraordinary sense of humor. She sent a lengthy letter, a mixture of professional advice and concern as a friend. It wasn't much, but it reassured me that eventually I could overcome this crisis.

We also called my former therapist from Venezuela, Irene Gutierrez, who was in the process of immigrating to the United States. She was taken aback by what I told her over the phone.

"Lisbeth, your problem was always clinical depression. Where is this international conspiracy delusion coming from?"

"Irene, they don't believe me, but they are on the phone, with microphones all over. They are listening to everything I say."

"I am convinced that thought disorders happen to smart people. You have intelligence on your side. Use it to separate reality from delusion. I know you don't believe in angels, but I think it is about time you do." This enraged Zoë.

"The last thing we need is a religious delusion. What we need is a psychiatrist and quickly," Zoë said.

"We called Dr. Silver again, but he said, "It's summer. They are all playing golf."

"What is this, a fucking Shrink Open in Southern Ontario?" Zoë snapped.

More than a month had passed without adequate medical care, but I wasn't alone. Dianne Duffy, the psychiatric nurse, visited twice a week. Her orange hair and her Irish accent entered my dim living room before she did. She checked the medication, played a bit with Saul, asked him questions, and routinely asked me what I had for meals in the past days. Additionally, Jussef took good care of me. And Zoë called daily. She was frustrated and tired, but she never left me alone. My friends from Venezuela wrote letters restating their love and their good wishes. They all said many wonderful things to me that I still cherish.

I was completely dissociated when I finally saw a psychiatrist at the Credit Valley Hospital's Outpatient Clinic. In my mind, thousands of people had gathered outside the hospital's doors to see me come in as a drug addict and criminal, and many more watched on TV from the comfort of their homes.

The hospital was full of TV cameras, and journalists reported on the mysterious immigrant from Venezuela with a scarred face live from the entrance hall. I was infamous. For the first time my identity would be revealed.

I pressed my back against a wall, waiting for my name to be called. I cried because I understood how far out of my mind I was.

*

I HAVE FEW MEMORIES of my first appointments with Dr. Christopher Doyle, the young psychiatrist fresh from residency who took my case. What I do remember is that Dr. Doyle was hot, as in sizzling hot. Tall and handsome, his face lit up with a broad smile. Always professional, he never gave any indication that he knew the effect his looks had on me. And I never gave it to him either.

I arrived back home one day and told Jussef, "Esto no va a funcionar, ese tipo está demasiado bueno. I'm going to end up having sexual fantasies about my shrink."

"Listen, Lis." Jussef's voice rose a bit too high. "This is the only psychiatrist in Mississauga at the moment. All others are either playing golf or hiking in the Algonquin. I can't drive you back and forth to Toronto for appointments. We don't have a choice."

"Enjoy the view," was Zoë's advice.

Other women professionals started wandering around the outpatient clinic, making small talk with the front desk ladies. They all wanted to talk to and see the new psychiatrist. I was proud of the guy.

"That's my doctor," I said whenever I caught one ogling Dr. Doyle.

I commented on this in one of my casual phone conversations with Irene. She said she was happy the doctor was pleasing to the eye. Maybe in male company, I would finally open up about my past.

"There will be no peace in your mind until you let go of what's holding you from being happy," Zoë agreed.

He did try to make me speak once. He even tried to hypnotize me, but I put up a fight. "I don't want to go there." Not that I wouldn't talk. I talked my head off. I simply didn't go where it hurt. Not with Irene, not with Dr. Doyle. I could never bring myself to chase down the giant cockroach.

It took Dr. Doyle several appointments to give me a diagnosis. He was certain that I had a late onset of Bipolar Type II and that at the peak of the manic cycle, I had developed a paranoid psychosis. His statement differed from what Zoë had diagnosed. She said it was a paranoid psychosis, but she had never mentioned bipolar disorder.

"Bipolar is characterized by mood swings from depression to mania. That's why sometimes you feel hopeless and other times exhilarated," Dr. Doyle said from his armchair in the consultation room in the hospital.

"I haven't felt exhilarated in a while. It seems all I do is cry," I interrupted.

"A typical individual with bipolar disorder swings in noticeable cycles from depression to mania. It used to be called Manic Depression," he continued.

"A doctor in Venezuela a long time ago said I was manic-depressive. I didn't like that."

"Bipolar II is trickier because the lines between depression and mania are not so sharply defined," Dr. Doyle said. "In your case, you developed a psychosis at the peak of the mania. We hope it was an isolated episode."

I felt relieved. It had a name and could be treated. I asked him if he could help me manage it without digging into my past. All I wanted was to learn to live with what I had. The way I saw it, I gravitated between a feeling of hopelessness and an unstoppable energy to constantly arrange my life in Canada. Looking for a job, making a home, adjusting to a new country, culture and reality. It didn't seem like mania; it was the stress of immigration.

I avoided reading about bipolar disorder for fear of copying symptoms I didn't have. Little by little, medical terms learned in therapy slipped into our domestic vocabulary: hallucinations, delusions, dissociation, psychosis, grandiosity, and self-reference - the idea that everything said or heard referred to me.

Dr. Doyle put me on a combination of antipsychotics and antidepressants. The antidepressants helped with the little obsessions I had developed during the breakdown. I was too concerned with my body odors; I thought my genitals smelled so bad that everybody noticed. I catalogued our books. The symptoms were under control in about a month, although it would take years for most to disappear.

The antipsychotic medicine took longer to kick in. In a few weeks, fights with giant cockroaches disappeared, but I continued to feel smaller roaches crawling on my body. I still heard my mother's voice in my head. The guilt and fear of having caused damage to my son prevailed.

Dr. Doyle taught me how to use the environment to come back and ground myself. He taught me to focus on my senses, to establish contact through my skin.

How does the air feel?

How is the light in the room?

What color is the chair?

With Dr. Doyle's exercises and medication, in a few weeks, I learned to return to my skin, and, to this day, I have remained in reality.

I communicated his teachings to my family, and Jussef and Ramón started the gentle touch method. If I suddenly developed a vacant look in my eyes and didn't respond to words, they would touch my arms softly, and with that simple gesture, they would bring me back to reality. When my mother's voice tormented me, all I needed was my son's small hand on my arm or my husband's gentle touch. This language of gestures separated the horrors of my childhood from my beautiful life in Mississauga, Ontario. My mother wasn't there, and she couldn't harm me again. Their soft hands protected me.

I never told Dr. Doyle or my family what I heard inside my head when I seemed to fade away. I made jokes about being wired up in the attic. Jussef and Ramón, now all too aware of my psychosis, would join me in the teasing. If somebody passed gas at the table, they would say, "Smile! You're on Candid Camera!"

The situation didn't change radically, only enough to be functional. I took care of my sons, was not an immediate threat to them, took my medication as directed and developed a routine with which I could live. The residual symptoms of psychosis lingered, though. The news still referred to me, for instance. And whenever I met with the group of Venezuelans in Mississauga, I felt they all made fun of me—that I was their joke. I broke dishes by the pound. Once, I told this to Dr. Doyle, ashamed of myself for being such a drama queen. He said that many people do break dishes and are not mentally ill. It's just how some people vent their frustrations.

*

IT WAS NOW THE middle of winter and as a hypomanic, I enjoyed everything with the fascination and thrill of a first kiss, even at 30 below. After one snowstorm, I wrapped Saul in his snowsuit like a hallaca[3], and bundled myself up. I could hardly move with two pairs of leggings, snow pants, boots, two long shirts, a coat, and a knit cap. I put Saul on a blue sled and grabbed the cord to pull him out of our ground floor apartment through the patio door. I lifted my knees to my chest; then, I let my feet sink deep into the snow. My efforts were halted by the white pack that covered every surface of the rental

[3] A Venezuelan dish wrapped in plantain leaves, similar to Central American tamales.

complex around Lake Aquitaine. Then, we went back home to drink cups of hot cocoa.

When we first moved to Canada, I experienced a particularly bad blizzard. I saw a woman walking backwards against the wind, which was probably too strong for her eyes. She moved slowly, lifting one leg at the time, leaning backwards as she lowered the leg and lifted the other, then stopped, exhausted. She seemed to be propelled forward and farther away from wherever she had intended to go. The next day, people moved around on skis, and snowplows made way for cars in the parking lot. I stayed indoors, with my hands around a cup of coffee, transfixed by the whiteness outside my window. Now, more than a year later, I was excited to be in it.

Once we hiked in Halton Hills in Milton, Ontario to a clearing in the woods and found a pile of chopped wood and a fire going. People sat down around the fire to enjoy hot cocoa from their thermoses and conversations with fellow hikers. We learned about s'mores that way, by watching the Canadians combine crackers, hot marshmallows, and chocolate chips while we sat in front of the fire. The park rangers also sold bird food at the gate. I fed small wrens from my hand while Saul and Ramón ran around looking for animal tracks. The light feet of the birds and the soft flapping of feathers in my hands brought a smile to my face and lightened up my sorrows.

Step by step, one winter at a time, I needed fewer pills (a hundred milligrams of antidepressants and one and a half milligrams of antipsychotic to call it a normal day). It felt I had a happy life. Our small group of friends expanded to include young families with children Saul's age. Little children ran in and out of the ground floor apartment all day. I loved the normalcy. Jussef worked all day, and I juggled my part-time substitute teaching assignments with Saul's activities, which included sitting with him at the curb waiting for the school bus to arrive. It was our thing, and it didn't cost me a bit to please him.

*

I LANDED A JOB as an occasional substitute teacher – supply teacher, as they call it in Canada. An automated system would call me in the evening to issue an assignment in a hard to find location. Each morning, I drove around Southern Ontario, stopping frequently to read maps. When I finally found the location, I realized I had arrived in the parking lot of a hospital, a group home, or a medium security correctional institution for juveniles. I learned then that wherever children were under state custody, there were schools to serve them and teachers who often needed days off.

I entered these small, self-contained classrooms, exuding my insecurity like a scent. When the assignment was inside a regular school, the specific classroom was segregated from the rest of the school and had different times for recess and breaks. These students were not allowed to mingle with the general population. Independently of the type of facility, the few students in the classroom were angry at the world and could smell my fear and inexperience.

Once, in a middle school in Milton, I found three students in a separate building. One student remained in a corner; another one punched anything within sight; the third, a girl, talked openly about sex. The oldest was 13. Although I spoke English fluently, conversing with street savvy teenagers became a challenge. I didn't know street English or sex jargon. I was naïve in that sense. That morning, I heard the girl telling one of the boys that she would give him a BJ if he paid enough. I asked her what it was.

"You don't know what a BJ is?" The girl answered with a question.

"OK Ms. C, here is your new word "B-J," she said while slightly punching the boy in the arm.

"Repeat your new word," commanded the one in the corner as the three of them burst out laughing. During lunch break, I asked a teaching assistant what "BJ" meant. She wanted to know where I had heard the word, and I told her what had happened. I drove back home that afternoon on the 401 laughing to myself. When Jussef returned home that night, I told him, "I need to find a new job."

*

WITH A SECOND INCOME for our family and Ramón starting high school, we settled into our comfortable, new immigrant life. We started to put numbers together to buy a house. I left Saul in daycare whenever I had one of my part-time, substitute-teaching assignments. Sometimes I took odd jobs with Community Living Mississauga, providing respite for families with children (adult or young) with special needs. It wasn't glamorous, but this is how I began to live in Canada.

We expanded our small circle of friends to include Elsa and Victor from Peru, Cristina and Manuel from Mexico, and Patricia Berger and her husband from Guatemala, all professional, hard-working immigrant couples like us. With all my new acquaintances, I opened up about my medical condition. Friends who already knew me told me I didn't need to tell everybody about it, only when it was pertinent to the conversation. And it was true, I didn't want it to seem that my mental illness was the only thing I had to talk about.

Dysfunctionality lingered in our household despite our best efforts to adjust. I took my medication as indicated and did most of the exercises Dr. Doyle suggested. Zoë provided fundamental support from afar. From time to time, a dark shadow hovered over our otherwise nice life. It was always something small, something insignificant—a comment somebody made, news on the TV, Ramón not doing his chores.

For instance, I thought I saw a hairbrush on my bathroom vanity; a white brush made by the now extinct brand "Stanhome" (or was it "Tupperware"). It was about fourteen-inches long and four-inches wide, plastic from the time we discovered the domestic uses for polymer. I saw the hairbrush and started screaming angrily at it. I spent the whole afternoon complaining about my hair, how I couldn't find a hairdresser that understood my hair, which escalated into an out of control fit that ended with broken dishes, cussing, and slamming doors. Each time, those close to me wondered what they had done. It was my mother's brush, the one she used to detangle my hair and it lived in my memory with the endurance of its plastic lineage, and no amount of antipsychotic medication or therapy would ever eradicate it from me.

Non-Believers

I WAS RAISED CATHOLIC, but I became a non-believer while still young. Although I didn't care much for the sacraments, my husband still did. We decided he had the right to baptize Saul, who by then was four years old. Our main issue: choosing godparents.

Our situation was still mobile, so we had to choose godparents from long-term friends and relatives. My husband chose one of his brothers as the godfather. I called Zoë and asked her to please honor us by accepting the role of my son's godmother. She was the only friend who was closer to me than any other relative and could be with us in Canada though she wasn't Catholic.

"Of course, that'll be great. It'd be wonderful to have the kids together again and see how much they've grown," she said on the phone.

A few days later, though, she called, curiously asking questions about baptism: "Rob told me it was a big deal for Catholics. You know I'm Jewish, right?"

"Yes, I know. There are a few things you need to be aware of, but you already do those things because you are a good person. Most religions are about the same. What's important is to be a good person to others," I said. She still had more questions for me.

I told her about the sacraments, baptism, the original sin, St. John the Baptist, and how water is the symbol for rebirth. I told her it is important for Catholics to have somebody who can guide their children's spiritual journey. I did my best to draw from my strong catechism and religious education, but I couldn't pull from my faith for I had none. A smidgen of belief in a higher being still lived within me, but it was a fading conviction.

For me, there was no difference between a Catholic, a Jew, a Muslim or a Buddhist; a good person can guide anyone, and she was the best person I knew. In another conversation, she reported to me that her boyfriend had told her that Catholics throw big parties for baptisms and invite people from all over the place to celebrate.

"We aren't going to do any of that," I assured her. We couldn't afford a big party. It would be the four of us, my brother and my mother-in-law, my sister-in-law with her husband and young son, and Zoë's family.

"It's important to Jussef that the kid is baptized," I told Zoë.

We decided on St. John of the Cross, in Meadowvale, Mississauga for the ceremony. We purchased nice clothes and a beautiful gold necklace with a cross pendant for Saul, and keepsakes to send to friends and relatives. We selected a restaurant at which to celebrate immediately after, and we wore ourselves out cooking for guests for the day before the baptism.

Zoë arrived from New York with her boyfriend and her child. My sister-in-law arrived with her husband and child from Montreal. Except for my brother and mother-in-law who flew in from Caracas and stayed with us in the apartment, the rest went to hotels because our place was too small. On Saturday, the godparents attended training in the church, and then we all returned to the apartment to share a few moments together.

My sister-in-law couldn't find her way to the apartment. The drive took her an hour and a half from a hotel in the neighborhood. My paranoia set in. I thought she was meeting with all those other Venezuelans who had made fun of me.

"How is the environment here?" she asked my brother-in-law when she arrived. I lowered my eyes and pretended I didn't hear. I pressed on, offering finger foods, making small conversations and trying to be a good host, while feeling observed and scrutinized by her and my mother-in-law. Before the guests went to their hotels for the night, I reminded everyone of the plan to meet the next day for brunch at the apartment before heading to the church.

*

I WOKE UP early to cook and set the table for eight adults, one teenager, and three small kids. To my surprise, the neighbor and her little daughters had also invited themselves. Theirs was the ground floor apartment across the parking lot from ours. The children were used to coming back and forth. I would sit in the back porch and see Saul playing with the girls on the other side. Likewise, the girls' mother could see from her porch the girls playing with Saul on this side. We had taught them to yell for attention whenever they wanted to cross to the other side only a few yards away.

That day, the three girls entered our living room via the back porch. The little girls smelled the feast and asked for food, while the older girl headed for the bathroom. I thought it was comical, except their mother arrived looking for the girls, and seeing that there was food, decided to stay. My mother-in-law, so ready to judge, was livid because I had such low-class friends. I was gracious through the whole ordeal unlike Zoë who threw more than one dart at them. My mother-in-law blamed me: "You could have been more selective."

*

A WEEK BEFORE my in-laws' arrival, I had scanned our cookbooks and selected the meal I was going to cook. Jussef pointed out what he liked and what would be impossible to prepare without help. I went to the Arab grocery and bought the ingredients, carefully selecting the best possible meat and vegetables and asking the store clerks questions about preparing the dishes.

Two days prior to the baptism, I hunched over our kitchen table rolling grape leaves stuffed with rice and ground meat, carefully arranging them inside a deep pot, and putting all my best effort in the preparation of the complicated *yabbra.* On the morning of the event, I cooked the grape leaves over a bed of fatty meat in water with lemon juice and minced garlic and served it on a plastic tray - the only one I had that was wide enough to hold the short tower of rolled leaves. I also served *kibbeh*, for which I kneaded the extra-lean meat with ice cubes, gradually integrating wheat and onion juice, then layered it inside a baking dish and stuffed it with a mixture of more ground beef and nuts. I used images from the computer to imitate the intricate pattern of diagonal cuts on top of the *kibbeh.* I placed those on the table with the *full*, broad fava beans with chopped tomato, parsley and a dressing of garlic, olive oil, and lemon juice. On a platter, I displayed *labneh* (hard yogurt), *baba ganoushj* (eggplant dip) and *hummus* (chickpea dip), and pita bread to go with them. We had braided cheese, which Jussef's aunt from Montreal had sent in advance, and *lahim biajeen*, a sort of Arab pizza with lamb meat and spices, which I had bought from the grocery. I so much wanted it to be a decent meal.

I arranged all these foods on our kitchen table, which only sat four. We had to take turns eating. I wasn't an expert at entertaining, but I stretched everything I had to make a good memory for everyone. My mother-in-law pelted me with disapproval.

"Look at the serving dish," she pointed out. "Too much lemon on the *yabbra*," she said later.

"The *kibbeh* is dry, and the *full* is soupy."

At each one of her comments, I felt heat boiling up from my guts and sitting up in the middle of my chest.

The uninvited guests finally left and, after cleaning, it was time to get ready to go to church. My husband got ready first, while I got little Saul dressed and supervised Ramón. The rest took turns. Zoë walked out from the bedroom, wearing a flowery summer dress. My mother-in-law instantly examined Zoë from head to toe. To my amazement, Zoë looked at her in the eye, before scanning the woman from head to toe in the same rude manner.

"I didn't know we were in a dress-up contest. You told me it was not a formal affair." This is how Zoë taught me to serve my mother-in-law matter-of-factly.

When it was my turn to get dressed, my mother-in-law followed me into the walk-in closet. Suddenly, I was reminded of the camera eye from my crisis. How many times had I hidden inside this same closet when I felt people observing me, wanting to know even the color of my panties? It wasn't only my own mother's close surveillance I feared, but also my mother-in-law's toxic judgement.

"Can I have some privacy, please?" I asked.

"Oh, I just want to see how you fit inside those pants, being as large as you are." I failed to react. I let her stay as I changed, embarrassed and humiliated.

We arrived early at the church, and I moved quickly to talk to the priest. "My friend, the person I have chosen as a godmother, is not Catholic," I said in the best tone of voice I could muster.

"It doesn't matter," he said. "We all have Jesus as our Savior."

"That's the problem. She is Jewish by birth, but she doesn't practice because she is agnostic."

"Now, I have a problem with that, but let me ask you first, why do you want her to be your son's godmother?"

My eyes welled up immediately. "She saved my life, and she is the best person I know. If I ever fail my son, I know she will be there not only for him, but for both my children."

"She can stand with us by the baptismal pool; I can acknowledge her, but I cannot recognize her as the godmother."

I wiped my tears with a Kleenex. "That's symbolic enough for me, Father. Thank you."

I communicated this quickly to my husband, Zoë, and my brother-in-law. They all seemed to be fine with it. It was important for me that she would be allowed to be there, be honored with the role of godmother. My own godmother never taught me how to pray, but she showed me that large families could be healthy and live in harmony with respect for each other. She taught me how to serve food at a beautifully dressed table in appropriate dining clothes and sustain light conversations. My godparents' home was a respite. I wanted Zoë to be a respite for my sons.

Ours was a communal ceremony. The assembly included about 30 groups of parents with their babies and godparents standing in rows in front of the altar. The priest blessed them all at the same time. We were neither the humblest nor the best-dressed party of the communal baptism. However, I continued to cringe at my mother-in-law's comments about the way we were dressed. My friend Cristina and her husband showed up to celebrate with us at the church. They were dressed in their Sunday best. This didn't sit well with my mother-in-law, who yet again mumbled in Spanish, "Malvestida."

Godparents carrying the babies walked to a large candle near the altar to light the little flames in their hands. My little son was delighted that he was old enough to carry the candle by himself. With my brother-in-law and Zoë by his side, Saul's eyes sparkled with joy. His cheeks were rosy with the heat of summer inside the church, and a simple gold cross hung from his chest. Zoë's daughter wiggled from her mother's hand because she wanted to touch the candle too.

Back in our pews, my mother-in-law pulled a gold chain from her purse and proceeded to change the gold medal we had given Saul for a much more expensive-looking one and told him in front of us, "This is better." I felt as if somebody had thrown cold water on my face, and the feeling that I was holding more than I could bear crept up into my chest again.

At the same time, Zoë's daughter asked, "Who's that?"

"Who?" Zoë replied.

"The one bleeding on the cross," the girl answered in a hushed voice.

Zoë's eyes and mine met and we muffled a giggle. "That's Mr. Jesus. It's a long story, and I can't tell you about it now," she answered. I knew then that it was going to be a good story.

At the baptismal pool, parents, godparents, and relatives were called up by the child's name. My husband and I, Saul, my brother-in-law, my mother–in-law, and Zoë with her daughter, all approached the birdbath-like pool. The priest proceeded with the ritual of cleansing my angelic son from his original sin by pouring holy water on his head and drawing a cross on his forehead with oil.

After, we took group pictures. Zoë and I sat at the center of the front row – she in her shoulder-level dark hair, print dress and flat shoes, and I, in a light blue pant and top set; Saul and her child rested on our laps. Ramón stood to my left, looking at my mother-in-law, who stood next to Zoë. As usual, my mother-in-law looked impeccable with her short hair highlighted in golden strips, a solid brown top with a fine, long necklace, a printed skirt and four-inch pumps. In the back row, from right to left stood my brother-in-law, Rob, Jussef, and my friend Christina and her husband. At the far right side of the picture frame stood Jussef's sister and her family, as if intentionally detaching themselves from the group.

Seeing myself in the photo next to Zoë surrounded by our children and many family members, one would think that we had shared a long line of life events together. Yet it was the first time Zoë participated physically in one of my life events. After I heard the camera click, I reached for her hand and squeezed it.

*

AT THE ITALIAN RESTAURANT, we sat on the patio because the weather was ideal: sunny and in the low eighties, with a soft breeze. There were metal patio tables with umbrellas and no tablecloths. We ordered pizza for the children. My sister-in-law ordered whiskey and casually mentioned, "There is nothing better to order."

At the table, my sister-in-law and her husband announced that they had chosen Jussef to be their son's godfather. He was delighted.

My mother-in-law leaned over to her and said, "Just make sure it's an individual ceremony, would you?" It heated me with anger. They continued to be inconsiderate, not only to me but also to my friend and to my husband and child. They did not care that they were attacking their own blood.

After dinner, we drove back home in separate cars. Jussef and his mother drove together in his car. Later, he told me she said, "Oh, Jussef, I haven't seen such a hick baptism since Olga's son was baptized." Olga was her maid of over twenty years. I drove back with Zoë in her rental car, where she complimented my food and congratulated me once more on the event. She dropped me at the apartment, and we said good-bye.

Several more days of my mother-in-law's visit followed. Self-referent thoughts found their way into my head. There was a conspiracy between my in-laws and the Venezuelans in Mississauga. Nightmares of cockroaches creeping up my body once again woke me at night. I remember being drenched in sweat and crying. Jussef woke up to hold me and calm my suffering.

We let his mother erode us. It was expected of me to take her shopping and show her around. All the while, she and the voice in my head bombarded me with negative comments.

My mother's voice, too, began playing like a broken record.

"Carolina, you are nothing without me," the voice would scream.

"Leave me alone, please," I pleaded.

"When I die I'm going to pull your feet at night," the litany continued. "Maldito sea mi vientre que parí a esta perra," said the voice. "Esa muchacha e mierda nació pa' puta."

The day my mother-in-law left, I had to see the doctor. He immediately increased the antipsychotic dose, and I felt like I had been punished twice, once with my in-laws' presence and a second time by medication.

*

I HAD GONE THROUGH the rituals and traditions once more, trying to keep inside the marked path, where the signs pointed. I gave birth to Saul within the boundaries of a very traditional Arab family, but my in-laws were no better than my own blood. They made a big deal of all those milestones in their children's lives, but there wasn't a stronger faith in them or more respect for their sacred symbols. We were all actors. Everyone was phony.

When we finally talked on the phone again, I asked Zoë if she had a chance to see the things I had always complained about when referring to my in-laws.

"That woman is a gossipmonger; stay away from her as much as you can," she said.

"I don't know why she hated my food. I tried so hard." I let out a sigh.

"You are an excellent cook. Everything was delicious. It must have taken you all week to cook those foods. I appreciate the effort you put into entertaining us," she assured. At least someone appreciated my humble table made with love. I didn't care anymore if my mother-in-law and sister-in-law didn't think much of my food. It had been great, and I had been validated.

*

WE BOUGHT OUR first home on Dunnview Court – a two-story, brick townhouse at the end of a row of four. Dunnview Court was a short cul-de-sac in Mississauga, ON, and the friendliest neighborhood I've ever been part of. After a snowstorm, one neighbor brought hot cocoa out to those stuck shoveling paths in the dark after work. My husband and I so enjoyed shoveling the snow that we defended our turn. One day, I took a bottle of Venezuelan rum and shared a little cup with each of the neighbors out shoveling.

We now had many friends, mostly parents with children Saul's age, with whom we gathered to celebrate our children's birthdays. Also, we counted on the growing group of Latino friends from Guatemala, Mexico, and Peru. We enjoyed our suburban life and doing small repairs around our home. I didn't push harder in the employment department and took the time to care for Saul. I still needed a handful of pills to keep my symptoms at bay.

The first spring in our new home, Saul and Elton, the son of our friends from Zaire, helped me plant a small, white flowering tree in a corner of our lot. I imagined the tree shading us from the summer heat during barbeques where friends' plates and frosty beer bottles collected on our new glass and metal table. While I dug a hole in the ground, the kids played with the dirt. They threw soil at each other and stomped on the ground around the tree roots. I opened the hose to water the soil and soaked the boys in mud, to their delight.

That same spring, we finished the Canadian immigration process. I wanted to take a picture with an attractive Canadian Mountie to celebrate the moment.

I asked a greying, retired officer nearby to take it. The four of us smiled, squeezed between the judge and the Mountie.

*

JUSSEF WAS CALLED in during a strike to work as a scab, although they don't call it that in the oil industry. It wasn't clear how he could refuse without losing his job. He was unaccustomed to working long shifts, which wrecked his sleeping pattern and fouled his mood. He had to be absent for two weeks at a time without a strike break in sight. He had three life insurance policies, fearful that a small mistake could blow up the plant where he worked. But the pay was good; our income doubled that year. We made advanced payments on our mortgage, saved money and finished work on the basement. Jussef took his first vacation in five years and we made a trip back home to Venezuela with our new passports.

The muggy air and the chaos greeted us at the airport, along with my parents' smiling faces. They looked shorter than I remembered. They had greyed considerably. I kissed my father on the cheek, and then my mother hugged me. I stiffened, repulsed by the gesture. They hurried us to an SUV taxi and we drove for two hours with my parents asking questions until we reached my hometown and childhood neighborhood.

The heat was oppressive. Fear and tiny cockroach legs crept over my body as I held my little son's hand and walked into the house of my nightmares for the first time in five years. I took stock: the porch with the old bench, the garden, and the stag horns hanging by the front windows. The living room was now in bright colors like a box of crayons. The spacious kitchen, with its avocado green refrigerator and tiles, was the same. The TV in the family room corner, the smell of my mother's perfume, the dark backyard, and the cockroaches lurking in every crevice were also the same.

We sat at the kitchen table. Some of my siblings had come to greet me. I opened my suitcases to give them their presents.

"¡Coño, se robaron los regalos," I cussed, noticing swift fingers in the airport had snatched many of the little gifts I had brought.

"Look at you. You are so grown," I said when I saw my nephews and nieces and hugged them.

"Carolina, por qué te pusiste tan gorda?" my mother remarked on my body.

"The good life I live," I answered swiftly.

"How are you?" I heard my father ask Saul in English. Saul tilted his head and smiled, but said little. Ramón grinned and answered their questions and enjoyed every moment of the reunion.

My mother showed me to the bedroom above the backyard. Just as I remembered, only the two front bedrooms and the living room had glass windows. The rest of the house had security wrought iron window designs but no glass. With a tropical climate, the house didn't really need windows to protect it from the elements. The backyard bedroom sat above a covered space that my father used for storage. It had the greatest concentration of cockroaches. I was tired and couldn't sleep, but Saul surrendered to the heat and the long trip and fell fast asleep. I cocooned myself with blankets despite the heat and lay on the bed, unable to move from the paralyzing fear of the cockroaches. I counted the days to our departure.

In the morning, my family treated me like a celebrity. They offered me the best of everything they had. Neighbors came by to greet me, and I visited some of them, too. For the most part, I stayed in the house, trying to adjust to the rhythm.

I had prepared my responses in case there was a confrontation with my sister or mother about the revelations I had made on the phone four years earlier. Not a word was spoken on the matter. I never dared to bring up the conversation. Not that there were many chances to be alone. The house burst with relatives and neighbors coming in and out.

I went to Margarita Island with my brother's wife and her children. It was as beautiful as ever with its blue beaches, the paradise of my dreams. However, I wasn't able to enjoy the trip in my mother's unbearable company. She brought one of my nephews with her. As usual, she felt the need to correct the child's every gesture, turning each moment into a nagging event: "Don't do this, don't do that, muchacho el carajo." Painful bits of images invaded my thoughts during the day, and I ended up withdrawing into a tight face and ill mood. On the day we had planned to take a boat to the nearby Isla de Coche, I decided to stay behind with little Saul and spend the day at a local beach. I was ready to leave when Jussef joined us, but we still needed to go to Caracas to visit his mother. By the end of our Venezuelan vacation, I was so emotionally drained, I swore I would not go back if I had to visit those two women.

*

WE FLEW BACK TO CANADA a few days before two airplanes hit the Twin Towers in New York. As another fall passed, I planted one hundred tulip bulbs on the north face of the townhouse in anticipation of spring. But we wouldn't stay long enough to see them bloom. Jussef accepted a call from a headhunter who had arranged an interview with an oil company in the United States. They sent tickets for our family to explore Ponca City, Oklahoma. He said yes to good money and the prospect of a successful career despite not liking anything about the dry, empty plains during our visit.

"Oklahoma?" asked Dr. Doyle. "That's church and BBQ every Sunday. As far as I know, it's very conservative there."

"Oklahoma? Where is that?" most of our friends asked.

"Ooooooklahoma, where the wind comes sweeping down the Plains. Oklahoma O.K," sang the neighbor next door. "That's all I know about it because of that old film."

"Oklahoma?" asked Zoë. "Why are you moving? Why now? You are doing fine where you are. You seem the happiest since I met you in Venezuela."

I said goodbye to my friends in Canada and tried my best to leave the door open in case things failed in Ponca City. Dr. Doyle reassured me that he would communicate with my future psychiatrist to make sure I had continuity of care. Against Zoë's advice, a crew of movers invaded our small house and put everything but our suitcases in a truck. I closed the door behind me and leaned on the front porch's bricks. I cried for the serviceberry tree and tulips I'd never see grow.

Migratory Bird

THE CRISP, WINTER EVENING air greeted us as we tugged our oversized suitcases around the almost empty parking lot of Tulsa International Airport in search of our rental car. Two hours later, we entered Ponca City.

"Is this a ghost town?" Saul asked from the back seat.

"No," we responded in a choir as if calming our own fears. "It's not a ghost town. People are inside their houses, probably eating dinner or already sleeping," I said.

Saul and Ramón kept looking through the car windows.

"The parking lots are empty," Ramón said.

"There are icicles on the trees," Saul said.

"It looks as if something really bad has just happened," said Ramón from the back seat. "The trees are fallen. There is ice everywhere, and there are no people. I mean there are ZERO people."

"Let's do something," said Jussef, his hands draped over the steering wheel. "We'll check into the hotel, go to sleep, and tomorrow, we'll explore our surroundings instead of drawing such ugly pictures in the dark."

The anticipation of the new beginning kept us tossing and turning all night as if there were sand in our beds. At dawn, Jussef drove to the refinery according to instructions, while the kids and I remained in the hotel and waited to explore. To pass the time, I took the kids to the hotel's breakfast, which was an assortment of glazed donuts. A sad banana and two oranges sat in a basket, coffee pumped out of a tall dispenser that coughed 100% Colombian when hit three times on the lid, syrupy orange and apple juices, sweet tea, Yoplait yogurt, Fruit Loops, an annoyingly loud waffle maker with its companion batter sitting next to it, and plastic forks with Styrofoam plates.

Heavy with the medication's effect and boiling inside my Canadian winter coat, I walked slowly from the hotel to the nearby E.M. Trout Elementary School, a short building with white linoleum floors, to enroll Saul. The land looked flat as a bedspread, no hills or mountains in sight. At the school's front office, nobody asked if we spoke another language at home. We had Canadian passports, and that seemed to be enough. I squinted at the enrollment form in front of me, adjusting my vision, and I checked African-American in the ethnicity box. The woman standing next to me looked me from top to bottom and said, "You ain't Black."

"That's only half true, but then there is no box for me," I answered.

"How come?" the secretary asked.

"I am a Black Hispanic," I said.

"I thought you were Canadian. I mean this is a Canadian passport, isn't it?"

"It is indeed. I'm Canadian, but I'm a Black Hispanic. There is no box for 'Other.'"

"Is White Hispanic all right with you?"

If I were in my homeland, my response would have been "mujer morena, de sangre caliente, loca y con las uñas afuera." Instead, I answered mildly, "No, ma'am. I don't want to be contrarian, but I'm not White. I think it goes without saying."

"What's up with all the ice and broken trees?" I asked, moving the conversation along.

"Oh, we were hit by an ice storm a week ago," said the principal who had suddenly appeared through a door in the back of the front office. He looked young and dressed sharply. "It brought down power lines. Some of us were without power or water for five days. We are just now coming back to school." He then turned his attention to a child sitting by his office door. The office was decorated with apples: Apples on his desk, apple print paper strip bordering the top end of the wall, and apple shaped key holder.

Saul was now in school all day, and Jussef was reporting to work. Ramón had to wait a few days before the new semester began. So Ramón and I used the time to explore. The entire place did look like a disaster area in the daylight. Crews chopped down tree limbs. Trucks cleared debris, and firefighters inspected for safety. The ice melted fast.

A loud alarm went off at noon on the Thursday after our arrival. I couldn't tell what was happening, but the noise deafened me. Ramón and I took the hotel stairs and reached the lobby in no time. Downstairs, everything looked normal as people went about their daily business.

"What's that?" I panicked.

"Oh, that's the tornado alarm. It's every Thursday at noon," said the front desk clerk, a young woman in jeans and T-shirt.

"Well, you should post that information in every room. That thing scared me."

"Is this your first time here?"

"Yes. We just moved here Monday."

"Bless your heart. Get used to it, ma'am. That's part of the landscape. We have nasty tornadoes in the area."

"Lovely."

At first impression, the town's population seemed pretty homogeneous: Native Americans, white folks, and the occasional Latino like us. I didn't see any African Americans during the first month. Looking closer, there were population divisions not obvious to the naked eye. There were the Poncas, the Native American tribe that had settled in the area in the 1800s, and the rest of us – company employees or third party beneficiaries of the oil and cattle wealth of the town. The wealth seemed to skip the Poncas.

The first month, we took sightseeing trips on the weekends to historical landmarks and state parks. We drove across the Plains to Arkansas City, Kansas to the point of the 1889 Land Run and then drove the 22 miles south back to Ponca City. I fell asleep during most of the day trips with the chemicals lingering in my brain. We visited the Marland Mansion, an Italian village built by E.W. Marland before his financial decline and before a political career that led him to become Oklahoma's first Democratic governor. We walked down the majestic corridors, listening to the echo of our steps on the cold marble floors while the volunteer docent told us Ponca City's history and of its well-known oil company.

"Marland," the docent continued, "was good at finding oil but not at making money."

"It seems like he made good money. Look at this ceiling," I whispered in Ramón's ear.

"But he got caught in a game of lending and borrowing and they kicked him out of his company. Marland Oils became Conoco Oils," said the docent. "He lived in the house for only one year before he went bankrupt."

Two months after we arrived, Conoco 76 merged with Phillips 66 from nearby Bartlesville, the town in Terrence Malick's film *To the Wonder*, to form ConocoPhillips. We visited more beautiful facades like these – almost abandoned downtowns with early 1920s architecture. In the neighborhoods, the Art Deco splendor of the 20s disappeared and Ponca City was remarkably suburban. One could not tell we were in the middle of The Plains.

After we left the mansion, I felt uncomfortable in my clothes. Sweat ran down my arms and my skin itched relentlessly – side effects. I met Dr. Hamilton, who kindly adjusted the meds to a bearable dose. Dr. Doyle had been in contact with him and explained that he had increased the doses to help me cope with an international move. The consequences were already obvious. Milk started pouring from my breast six years after I stopped breastfeeding my youngest son. With my fallopian tubes tied, there wasn't a chance I was pregnant again. An emergency CAT Scan revealed no tumors in the pituitary gland. The family doctor explained the lactation was a side effect of the antipsychotics—yet another gift.

*

WE MOVED FROM the hotel to a house that had seen better days. Our neighborhood was on the outskirts of town on a dead end street. The yards were spacious with manicured lawns. Cows pastured just across the street from us. Deer and wild turkey walked on the front yard at night. In the path of migratory birds, our patio served as a comfortable spot for bird watching, as all sorts of wonderful birds visited our backyard. City dwelling urbanites, we soon learned what skunks smelled like and to watch for snakes and scorpions at every corner.

I never had so much space to myself and had never to taken care of so much space. The cabinets were sticky with grease accumulated through years of neglect; weeds colonized our lawn. The two red bud trees at the front had suffered from the recent ice storm. The windows rattled whenever the train ran a few miles away. The light fixtures displayed a mosaic of outdated styles. The stains on the beige carpet reminded us of murder mystery novels, and something in the house gave us all allergies. The bathrooms and kitchen needed an update, and the walls needed new paint. The roof was in poor condition. The moving truck soon arrived with our Ikea furniture, Canadian cars, and misplaced identities.

"Caracas, Toronto, Ponca City. I think we took a wrong turn somewhere," I told Jussef one day while battling yard weeds. As I bent over to attack a dandelion, I saw a blue heron standing across the street from my house. "Are you lost?" I asked the blue heron, "Where is home, Blue Heron? Where do you and I belong? Why are you here? Why am I here? How do you know where is home when your entire life is a transition?"

I ran back to the house to look for a camera to snap a picture. As I approached the bird, it tried to move. One wing opened wide, but the other hung sideways. It would have flown home if it were not broken.

*

THE MILE LONG LIST of things to do around the house was enough to put Jussef in a lousy mood every Saturday morning. "If you want it done, find somebody to do it. I'm not going to do that." The truth is he didn't know how to fix things; he had to start by learning from the internet and library books. He took cues from the neighbors, but he felt he needed training even to clean gutters.

Films, which had brought Jussef and me together, weren't often available in the city's drive-in theater or the smaller, indoor screens that showed light comedies like *Super Troopers*. Instead, we pointed our lawn chairs to the north and admired the open country's night sky. We could see the Milky Way (or, Jussef could see it, since I was only able to make out a blur of lights). When a stellar show was announced on the weather news, we placed our telescope outside, trying to catch whatever was on display: a meteor shower, an eclipse, a satellite. We spoke in soft voices, reminiscing about the life we had left behind.

*

MY TN 2 COMPANION VISA didn't provide resident privileges. The emergency measures taken by the US government after the 9/11 terrorist attacks made it even more difficult to move through immigration. Without a Social Security Number or a work permit, I placed my professional goals on hold and helped my family adjust to their new lives as smoothly as possible. At 38, I felt beloved and committed to them. We had a lot at stake, but I knew eventually my inner feminist would need to shift priorities.

It was disorienting too. My inner urbanite felt lost. I preferred the light and remotely disconnected atmosphere of a bar's after hours. I loved cerebral art films, galleries, and museums. I missed friends popping up in my apartment at odd hours in Caracas or going out with a group of friends on late evenings in Canada. In Ponca, people invited me to Bible study. When I declined, they said they would pray for me. They didn't see the need to talk to me about anything else.

I used my time to improve my basic cooking skills with the help of the Food Network, which was always on. I developed a menu for each day of the week and each week of the year. A recipe box materialized on my counter, with an expanding collection of neatly printed and illustrated cards. From a metal napkin holder, cue cards reminded me of what chore to do each day of the week.

In Ponca, I had a choice of women-only clubs. Determined to fit in and find my way around, I joined the Newcomers, the International, and the Rosemary-Sage clubs. I asked for recipes and chatted with women with big, sprayed hair, bolo ties, long skirts, and cowboy boots, who spoke with a heavy Oklahoma drawl. Expats like me - English, Norwegian, Arab, South African and Latin American, all related to the oil corporation in one way or another also attended meetings. They dressed up and cooked as if competing against each other to see who could put on the best show.

Those women spoke about their husbands as one might talk about personal achievements. I felt like a bar of soap in a china cabinet. I had never been a drinker, but I would have welcomed a glass of wine to keep my hands from fidgeting and my mouth from spitting bullets. My second February in town, in one of these monthly social gatherings, I suggested bringing drinks to the meetings and maybe even bringing men to spice up things. The stunned silence made me feel as if I had said "suck a cock" aloud in church. I was immediately shunned.

I tried the Catholic Church. We started with the Spanish service and hoped meeting with the mostly-Mexican congregation would provide us with a sense of community. The small crowd consisted of a few long-term parishioners and a priest that looked and sounded like Cantinflas.

"He was Jesus first and then Christ, and here is the detail, and notice that he had a name earlier and then another." His nonsensical rumblings dragged us into slumber.

We switched to the English service. This went well for a few months until I tried to stop the flow of correspondence they sent home.

"Hi," I said over the phone. "I receive too much mail from you every month. I think it is a waste of resources. Please stop."

The priest on the phone wanted to know my name. I repeated it to him several times, but he said I did not appear on his list. I had to make him understand that I didn't use my husband's name. This seemed to offend him.

"Oh, Lord. Are you a modern-day feminist?"

I chuckled at the question before I told him about a warm place he could go for the rest of his eternity.

"Suck it up, Lisbeth," Zoë said to my whining. "You have to make friends. You need somebody to talk to besides your family."

"Where did you bring us?" I asked Jussef one afternoon, furious at him for selling himself to a powerful oil company. "I had a good life in Canada."

*

IN A CORNER OF OUR backyard, I hugged the Silver Maple. The children had gone to school after a long weekend, and I felt alone and disconnected. The garden became my refuge. As I dug in the dirt to weed and plant, I grabbed the soil in my hands, felt its rough texture, and smelled its musky aroma. I planted herbs and native flowers around the fence; the Black-Eyed Susan was my favorite with its bright yellow petals and dark center. I added several trees: Mimosa and October Glory in the front yard, a Chinese Pistachio, another Silver Maple, and a Hawthorn in the backyard. Each one had a shade bed underneath for more flowers and native plants.

With bricks, sand, and a rubber mallet, Jussef and I built a kidney-shaped edge around the flowerbed in the front. Then I collected rocks from the Kaw Lake and used them to accent my garden. I filled my well-worn hiking boots from Canada with soil to serve as planters for colorful annuals and placed them right next to my front door. An old straw hat became a bird nest.

Zoë agreed that moving to the United States had not been the best choice and that the timing was bad. Jussef and I had managed to pull ourselves together pretty well in Canada, but we had not fully appreciated that we would have to readjust more than once.

*

RAMÓN TOLD US stories of girls in school showing off their virginity rings, a piece of jewelry to prove to the world they were untouched. Also, he mentioned that some students purposely interrupted the science teacher to prevent covering evolution in class.

"We went backwards forty years when we took that plane," I told Jussef. Ponca City was too conservative for bipolar talk, and there wasn't a single soul

I could trust about the side effects of my medication that I had now taken non-stop for five years.

In those years, I had progressively gained 60 pounds, experienced blurred vision, involuntary leg movements and stiffening of muscles, had terrible stomach pains and either diarrhea and constipation, forgot things and had to use visual reminders, and was obsessed with cleaning. After I took the medication at night, I sank into a stupor and went to sleep like a rock. Sex disappeared from my line of thought and feeling, and Jussef lost interest. Sometimes I woke up at night drenched in sweat. He wasn't there at all.

I got up to take Saul to school each morning, successfully avoiding other parents. My tongue felt heavy, as if coming from the dentist appointment, and I feared it would betray me. My throat felt like sand paper, and I drank water constantly, which meant I had to stop to pee everywhere. My skin became even more sensitive to the sun. The medication was mighty powerful but still left bits of paranoid thoughts.

I desperately wanted to speak about these things, but calling long distance was expensive, and few friends had the means for that. Our friends from Zaire, Maxime and Frank, tried the hardest to remain in contact. They sent letters and pictures of the children, but we missed the warm connection that proximity provided. Only Zoë and I were seasoned in the art of correspondence. We had been pen pals now for 17 years.

"You need a friend, even if it is to bitch about Jussef," she kept telling me.

Through volunteering at Saul's school, I made more acquaintances, but they remained superficial relationships. We helped teachers make copies, shelved books in the school library, timed standardized tests and cross-country meets, and though we talked while doing these tasks, we never had the comfort of conversation. I envied the other mothers who had lived in town all their lives and had a network of similar minded women to raise kids together. They had a tribe, even if it was the far right, fundamentalist Christian kind.

"Go out and talk to people," Zoë said.

"What would I talk about besides recipes, children, and husbands? Those are the only safe conversation topics. Global warming, religion, national security, abortion, feminist issues—everything is off-limits. The worst censor is Jussef. Everything can jeopardize his position, or so he tells me."

I told Jussef that I planned to change my license plate frame to a pro-choice one. "Don't you dare," he said. "Half the managerial crowd in the refinery is Mormon. The other half is Baptist. I could lose my job over your political statement."

"Wow."

"Why can't you just play nice with the other wives?" he asked.

"What do you want me to talk about? Democracy and free speech?" I asked in sarcasm.

"Books are a safe topic," he said.

"Yes. I'd love to find somebody to talk to about Sonia Sanchez with," I said.

"Well, you can't remain anchored in college forever, Lisbeth." I felt the condescension in his voice.

"Yes, but I have to keep a sense of identity, or I am going to lose myself. You got a career. What do I have?" I was screaming now.

"You are not a Black poet/activist, carajo." He raised his voice.

"I ain't no fucking White Baptist wife either," I said with my hands on my hips. "Why can't we go back to Canada? We're trapped in the 50s," I said before slamming the bathroom door.

The sense of alienation was stronger when I thought about my condition as a secret I had to protect all the time. It wasn't easy to have a spinning, addled mind in a corporate town. I worried about breaking in front of my husband's boss' wife over a cup of coffee after school drop-off. I wondered what would happen if I suddenly shared, "I woke up last night hearing voices." I was sure that "This stupid anti-psychotic medication makes me sweat at nights as if I were going through menopause" was not a good icebreaker.

"How can I start a new relationship when I feel like I am keeping a secret?" I asked Zoë.

"It's not a secret. It's a wise omission. First, you find your bearings, get a good sense of where you are standing, then you can learn to trust that piece of information to somebody," she said.

I didn't want to go around telling people, "Hello, I'm your new bipolar/psychotic neighbor," but, at the very least, I wanted to be able to tell my son's teacher about my mental condition without fear of being banned from school grounds. Zoë was adamant about me keeping that information to myself. That made me angry because I had not committed a crime.

"Well, what good will it do? Keep a low profile and concentrate on adapting and making friends. The rest will come," she said.

I thought that at least Saul's teacher needed to know, so I told his second grade teacher one afternoon after school pick-up. I knocked on her classroom door.

"Mrs. Dingus. Do you have a couple of minutes? I need to talk to you," I said.

"Yes, Mrs. Coiman. How can I help you?" Mrs. Dingus offered a polite Mona Lisa face framed by long greying hair. Always dressed in a denim jumper and walking shoes, Mrs. Dingus stood as the model for the teacher I wanted to become one day – organized, calm, competent and concerned for her students. Standing in front of her by the chalkboard, I inhaled deeply and then started.

"There is something you must know. Something very personal. I'm mentally ill. Please, don't raise an alarm. I want you to know because we don't have family in this country, and we don't have many friends in town either. After all, we've been here for less than two years. My son's entire network of care is in this school. I want somebody to know in case there is an emergency at home. There is nothing to worry about at the moment, though. I am under the care of a good professional in town." I said all of this in one breath, but my eyes welled up fast, and I turned to look at the bright light coming through the window to my left.

"May I ask what exactly is your condition?" Mrs. Dingus asked without changing her expression.

"Five years ago, I was diagnosed with Bipolar Disorder. At the peak of my manic episodes, I have a tendency to develop paranoid psychosis," I explained in the least emotional tone I could use.

"Mrs. Coiman, you'd be the last person I'd think of as bipolar, let alone psychotic. You don't have any idea of the number of parents who've used those same words as excuses for abuse or neglect." Her words sounded like a beautiful reward to my efforts of maintaining normalcy in my house, but also as a reminder of how people saw the mentally ill. I exhaled the pressure I had been holding, finding comfort in the well-organized classroom and the smell of sharpened pencils in the air.

"The physicians who care for me did not present me with a written permission for misbehaving. I'm not crazy. I don't act the part or use my diagnosis as an excuse for misconduct." After thanking her for listening and for helping us educate our son, I walked into the principal's office.

Dark blue wallpaper with apples and yellow pencils bordered three walls. A floor to ceiling window on the north side opened to a view to the playground. The young and handsome principal, Mr. Edwards, whose coming out years later was one of the town's worst scandals since Marland married his adoptive daughter, listened sympathetically as I repeated the monologue. I gave him the name of my psychiatrist, his business card, and permission to contact anybody they considered necessary if they ever felt my son was in danger. I didn't do the same for Ramón. He didn't want me anywhere near his school.

"Thank you, Mrs. Coiman. I'll keep it in my Rolodex, but I know I'll never have to use it."

I walked back home through the streets of mowed lawns and brick houses lined by mature trees feeling proud of *coming out.* I looked up and noticed a flock of Canadian geese flying in a perfect triangle – migratory birds that had lost their way back home.

Rotating Clouds

FROM THE KITCHEN DOOR, I looked at the sky and saw a grey I didn't have a name for, a grey so powerful that it felt obscene, like the word *fuck*. The birds had all gone south, and there was two feet of malleable snow. Or was it 30 centimeters? I couldn't get used to the standard measuring system based on body parts. The white sat on the naked limbs of the trees, on the glass patio table, and on the chairs. I felt the days go by as if I were walking through a viscous curtain, as if my feet sank in gelatin, and I had to pull each foot up with a gargantuan effort.

I didn't know of any hills to take Saul tobogganing, so we spent snow-days at home. The little one grew more fascinated with the snow in Oklahoma than in Canada because it wasn't as frequent here where winters were usually brown and boring. Whenever as much as half an inch fell, schools closed, and the kids had fun making brown snowmen, as if out of a *To Kill a Mocking Bird* scene. But snow and winter had lost its fascination to me when we moved.

I'd been dragging since we arrived in the plains. In the States, the chemistry of my brain had not cooperated; I felt depressed most of the time with winter's weight on my eyelids. I wanted to sleep. I fell asleep on the sofa and dreamed briefly of a child making sand castles on a sunny beach, but woke up startled when the coffee spilled on my lap. "¡Coño!" I said to myself. The field across the street matched the hopelessness of the sky; I didn't know anymore where one began and the other ended.

It was the fourth day inside. I saw people in their pick-ups, skidding on the snow-covered roads. A small sedan entered the street, skidded, spun, and hit a mailbox. Soon, the neighbors came out, arguing and exchanging phone numbers with the driver. I watched the scene from inside. I didn't see the point of starting a conversation or trying to be friendly. Instead, I sat around the house and watched Saul play in the spacious yard.

I walked to the kitchen counter and found an orange and a persimmon, which are the only fruits one can find in Oklahoma at the beginning of January, unless one is willing to pay the price for a pound of California strawberries or put up with tasteless bananas from Costa Rica. Every import tasted like jet fuel or snow. Persimmons are native. In Oklahoma, one can count on oil, wheat, and persimmons.

I tested the persimmon's orange skin, soft like an overripe tomato. Then, I placed the fruit on a dish. I cut it in half and put a teaspoon next to it. I carried the dish to the armchair by the window where I could see Saul still playing in the snow, his cheeks rosy, his dark hair wet on his forehead. I took the spoon and dug into the tender, ripe fruit, scooping a bite and bringing it to my mouth. I closed my eyes to taste its sweetness. I looked carefully at the color: a bright orange with a silky texture. I tried to enjoy the fruit, but I thought of passion fruit, medlar, and guava - the flavors of my homeland. I told myself the mood had to go. I needed to do something to shake this sadness off my skin. I needed a job most of all. I finished the fruit and walked outside.

"It's time for hot cocoa," I called to Saul.

"And s'mores," he shouted back from the yard. One could always count on a child to brighten up a grey day.

*

I SLOWLY SETTLED into the sheltered corporate wife role and played by the rules. I invited Jussef's coworkers to splendid dinners at home. I attended the company gym. When I chatted with people, I made sure to always mention my husband's name, and for whom he worked. Jussef never wanted to play golf or go fishing, but he seemed pretty content that I had domesticized so well.

I became a brown, accented Martha Stewart, crafting presents for teachers and secretaries, making my own greeting cards to send to family and in-laws abroad, coordinating dinner parties for 12, tending to my garden, baking bread, and even making my own hard yogurt. For Christmas, I prepared little packages of homemade jam for my neighbors. I had the perfect children and the perfect drug cocktail to keep a sense of sanity.

We settled into a comfortable life that allowed for long vacations. The first trip was to New York for Zoë's wedding. Rob had moved into her house a year before she sent the email to all her friends announcing her engagement.

"Last night, Rob presented me with a simple ring. He asked me to marry him and I said *yes*," the email read.

Friends, people like me who had met Zoë during her travels, came from as far as Russia to Zoë and Rob's wedding in Manhattan. The simple ceremony took place in the basement of a synagogue and was officiated by a humanist, female reverend. Zoë wore a strapless, long white gown with embroidered yellow flowers all around the skirt. She said the dress had called her from the window of a consignment store. She was radiant in a white headband decorated with embroidered daisies over her black, short hair. She held her daughter's hand.

The guests helped themselves to disposable cameras provided on a table at the entrance. We had fun snapping pictures of one another that we later shared. After Rob and Zoë read their vows, he played the guitar for her, which initiated the party. The guests sang "Eight Days a Week" and danced into the night. Towards the center of the room, closer to where the band played, Zoë's intimate circle of friends danced and celebrated. I spotted Lisa Harrison in the crowd, whom I remembered from my previous trips to New York, and Ellie Nagler, one of the other two women I had met in Venezuela so many years ago. Although there were lots of casual introductions, I couldn't remember all the names. Running around the adult guests, a band of little kids chased each other, snapping pictures with the disposable cameras. Among them, my own little son and Zoë's daughter, Kathy, who had been the flower girl. We shared a table with Kathy's first grade teacher, who told us how Zoë had singlehandedly brought a music program into her school.

Most of those I talked to that night and the next day at a small celebration brunch for the out-of-town guests had one thing in common with me. They had been pen-pals with Zoë for close to or more than 20 years. They had met during one of Zoë's trips abroad, and their friendship later strengthened through letters and now emails. A woman from Virginia, whom Zoë met during a short vacation, spoke about her cheerfulness and kind spirit. All of us agreed that our lives were better because she had been part of it.

Jussef went back to Ponca City while I remained in New York for an extended vacation with my sons. I grinned for several days during walks around the wide avenues and between the city's many languages on each block. I took the boys to the Natural History Museum because it was Ramon's favorite. After a few hours, I left Ramón in the museum and took Saul with me to Central Park to meet Zoë and Kathy. We chatted for about an hour while we watched the kids play nearby. I wanted to stay with her in the fascinating city where I was sure I could find employment and fulfillment if I tried, but we had to say goodbye and go back to our lives. I congratulated her once more on her wedding, and I held her in a long embrace as I said good-bye.

The next day, we took the airplane back home to tornado alley.

*

WHEN THE TORNADO alarm went off, I watched the neighbors go out to admire the rotating clouds, which twirled over our houses in enormous multicolored towers. Jussef took the camera out. The air turned bright green, and the sky broke. Rain came down in buckets. Then, penny-size pieces of ice grew into golf balls. Hail descended upon us with fury.

Ramón grabbed a video camera and went out the patio door to film the gutters giving in to the weight of the ice. I felt a sense of urgency when the emergency radio kept telling us to look for shelter, but instead I stood by the living room window. Jussef stared at the television to learn about what was happening. Saul, only six then, knew exactly what to do. He went into the small coat closet and called all of us in.

"We have to go in the closet!" he yelled.

The four of us crowded inside for nearly ten minutes as what felt like a train tested the integrity of our home. The tornado had touched at the edge of town. We came out of the closet and noticed water dripping from the ceiling. Outside, neighbors were already assessing the damage. Ice had poured onto the streets and gardens. About a foot of white balls collected against the wall by our front door. My garden resembled a gigantic chopped salad. The glass table in the back yard was upside down and in pieces; tree limbs lay everywhere; the outside doors and most of the south looking windows had been hammered by the hail; the gutters were on the ground. Fortunately, we had good insurance to pay for all of the damage. We learned that even when the neighbors go out to look at a storm, one is better off taking shelter in the lowest part of the house.

*

WATCHING THE MAIL gave me hope and joy. I walked to the curbside mailbox in the predawn of social media in anticipation of news from those I had left behind. The flag down meant that I was missed, remembered. My heart leapt as a child in a playground. I opened a white envelope addressed to Mr. and Mrs. Awad. Inside, there was a card with two white doves holding a string of pearls with a delicate bouquet of roses in pastel colors. "Two hearts, two lives united forever in love." I flipped the card and read the invitation from Jussef's cousin to his wedding in Montreal.

Apart from learning to cook elaborate Arab dishes, I had also put a lot of effort into learning Arabic. I didn't make much progress with audiotape courses but had come to understand and respond to greetings and a few other words. I had also learned to grasp meaning from cues in gestures and tones of voice. With my piecemeal Arabic and presents for family and friends, we went to Canada.

We spent a few days with Cecilia and Nacho in Mississuaga first. While Cecilia and I talked, Jussef, Nacho, our two sons and theirs went to a baseball game in Toronto. Cecilia would have preferred for us to go to a casino in Niagara, but I wanted to just listen to her tell me about everybody we used to know and how they were doing.

First, Cecilia told me about how Ana had been so stoic in her fight against brain cancer. She had been determined to survive at least until her daughter could take care of herself, but now Carlos and their children were recovering from their grief and were doing well.

Cecilia had moved up the ladder in the Community Living agency where she worked assisting people with mental disabilities. Nacho had quit his warehouse job, trained as a massage therapist, and was on his way to building his own clientele for a small business that ran out of their home basement. The entire house had been updated to accommodate both the developmental and physically disabled adults they usually took care of.

The day before our departure, Cecilia and Nacho hosted a BBQ for us and invited several of our friends. Most of our Canadian friends came to visit us in their house. Seeing them again reassured me that I still had friends that cared for me, that I wasn't as alone as I felt in Oklahoma. For two hours, we joked, told stories, and tried to catch up with the events of the last couple of years. I wanted to hold on to them, stay in Ontario, and never go back.

Then we took our rental car and drove to Montreal. Paranoia set in as soon as I touched Quebecois soil. I felt eyes on me, scrutinizing my nail length, my hips, and the quality of my dress. I scraped together conversations with my in-laws. The day of the wedding, I sat at the kitchen table to watch a group of house helpers serve the splendid hors d'oeuvre. My mother- and sister-in-law sat next to me at the same table but spoke only in Arabic. I could only make out bits of their loud diatribe: *Venezuelan women*, *witches*, *promiscuous*. The looks of disdain they threw at me, the repetition of "venezuelii," all told me that I was being targeted.

One of the maids asked me later, "Are you Venezuelan?"

I moved to another spot in the living room, and soon my mother-in-law sat nearby repeating her performance with an older lady who looked at me sideways, as if in disbelief.

Before the reception, we stopped briefly at my sister-in-law's home, where my mother-in-law asked me, "So you understand Arabic, right?" and proceeded to insult me in Arabic. I couldn't make out one single word, but her tone, her gesture and the disgust in her face was translation enough. I felt eyes following me as Jussef and I danced at the reception. With my mind already racing with self-referent thoughts, I felt the cameras were stealing images of my facial expressions and behind, and knew these photos would later appear in newspapers across the nation.

The day after the wedding, the family gathered at a Syrian restaurant to celebrate Jussef's grandparents' 60th wedding anniversary. My mother-in-law flitted from one small cluster of women to the next, murmuring to each group, who then turned to look at me. If I tried to talk to somebody, my sister-in-law interrupted and made sure I couldn't have a decent conversation with one single person. I was exhausted.

"I am done with your family," I told Jussef when we got back to Oklahoma.

"But we only see them occasionally. How hard can that be?"

"You know what? That's your problem. Horrible as my family is, they never bother us. They are not allowed to spread toxicity around you because I set the limits straight from the beginning."

"What do you want me to do?" he yelled.

"I don't know what you are going to do, but you either have a serious conversation with your mother and sister about boundaries and respect, or they won't see my ugly face again. Not that they want to see me. Esas sólo quieren joder. They just want to bother."

Gossip kills, and it kills mentally ill people first. I never again called them, or remembered their birthdays, or sent a single greeting card. Jussef was free to invite them to our home or call, but he couldn't expect me to be social with them.

After the Montreal wedding, I sank into a psychotic crisis and needed to increase my medication. I disconnected from all media. I wrote only on paper and immersed myself in my garden as therapy. Nobody, not even the mother of the person I most loved in this world, was worth my sanity.

Falling Apart

JUSSEF GREW DOMINEERING and inflexible with money, demanding more and more savings, requesting that I do more things from scratch to minimize costs. I sank deeper into the housewife trap.

Holding a cup of coffee in my hands, I observed the bloom of the Crepe Myrtle in the backyard. The clusters of minute white flowers buzzed. Jussef entered the kitchen.

"Where were you last night? I asked him. "I woke up in the middle of the night because I was drenched in sweat and you were not in bed with me."

"I was sleeping on the sofa. I couldn't sleep well and I didn't want to bother you." He said softly.

"Which sofa? I walked around the house, but couldn't find you anywhere." I wanted to know.

"Maybe I was in the bathroom."

"Which bathroom?" I pressed on.

"Why are you grilling me?" He wasn't calm anymore.

"You weren't home last night. That's why."

"You're crazy." Jussef raised his voice.

"I already know that. What I didn't know is that it comes in handy for you to fuck around while I'm asleep, heavy with meds."

"Negrita, estás celosa." Jussef looked at me from above the rim of his glasses, pulled me into his arms, poking my neck with his long aquiline nose, and I melted, forgetting our disagreement.

The trick didn't work for long. We fought a lot. We shared a house but not a home. He abandoned our bed, and I gave up on intimacy with him since he allowed his mother and sister to berate me. It wasn't much of a protest with the antidepressant sitting on my libido and his disinterest. He complained that I let myself go, and that I didn't give him credit for the good things he did. He turned despotic.

"Come and clean this," he shouted from the bathroom once. On the tile floor was a bottle of spilled shampoo.

"Can you please pick up your socks from the floor?" I asked.

"You know what? I work full time. What do you do all day? Watch Food Network?"

I saw his reflection on the door mirror, looking at my naked body. A grimace of disgust. I felt ugly, obese. I exercised more and lost weight, but gained it back fast. The pills were relentless, but I wanted to be desirable to Jussef.

He punished me—took me to the worst bar in town on our anniversary, one of those dark joints where you don't want the lights on for fear of finding out what's crawling on the floor. At the bar, his attention was somewhere else. I danced alone, doing my best to repel the men who approached me.

When we drove back home, I complained to him about his behavior, how he had left me alone on our anniversary in a creepy joint. At 3 a.m., he screamed at me that I had become a bore. The argument escalated, and I unhinged. My heart pounded like knocks. I spoke fast and coarsely. I felt a current invading me from the stomach up to my brain. With tears drowning my face, I began to roar.

I failed to recognize the break; the deep voice screams should have been my clue. I punched the right side of his face. An uppercut followed, and soon I delivered a shower of punches – probably weak but fully-landed – from the right and left while Jussef crouched and took the beating until I calmed down.

"I'm sorry. I'm sorry. I'm sorry. Please forgive me," I cried and fell to my knees in front of him. We both cried.

I hurt Jussef. I didn't hurt him badly, and yet, how could I hurt the man who had adopted my son when I was a single mother? How could I hit the person who took a leave of absence to nurse me into recovery? The last thing I wanted to do was to abuse him. But I wasn't going to take his shit either. I wrote two letters: one to Ramón asking him to help with Saul, and one to Saul explaining that I had not abandoned him. I took $600 in cash, a suitcase full of clothes, my passport, and left.

I knocked on the door of an acquaintance, who allowed me to stay for the night.

Jussef caught up with me the next morning. First, he called me. Then, he arrived at the acquaintance's house in our red Ford Escort with the children in tow. In his customary plaid shirt and jeans, bespectacled and bald, he stepped out of the car, closed the door gently, and walked to the house where I had just spent the night.

"Un divorcio es un negocio," he said. "You got more to lose than I have. You'll lose custody of Saul because I can prove in court that you are mentally ill."

I went back. Silently.

Ramón was on his way to college now and wouldn't present a custody problem in case of a separation, but the fear of losing Saul weighed heavily. I realized I had surrendered total control of my life to Jussef. I didn't have a bank account. I was in a foreign country as an attachment to my husband's

NAFTA Treaty visa. I didn't have a Social Security number. I couldn't enroll in graduate school or get a student loan. I didn't have the right to work or to obtain custody of my children, and the house and the car were in his name.

*

JUSSEF KEPT COMING back home smelling of perfume. He flirted openly with blond women, but he never admitted to adultery.

I lied to myself. *It's all in my head. He is not cheating. He detached to cope with my mental issues.* I held onto that lie for years. The mental effort I put into tying up the loose ends instead of following what my gut was telling me added to the psychosis. One day I became so paranoid, I destroyed some of the letters Jussef had written to me when he was in Cincinnati, along with most of Zoë's letters.

Jussef asked me, "Will you even remember a few years from now that you once loved me?"

Despite our issues, I maintained the corporate wife façade, even entertaining Jussef's colleagues from time to time. During a little social, I ran into the bathroom and from the corner of my eye, I saw a plump woman, perhaps in her mid-forties, looking back at me in the mirror. She was brown, and a perfectly styled bob with blond highlights hid the left side of her face. She wore a bright green blouse over a black, knee-length pencil skirt, black pumps, pearls and gold jewelry. Very simple. Elegant for the plains.

I wondered who she was as I walked to the toilet and pulled down my panties from beneath my skirt. As I squatted, a bang of highlighted hair fell on my face. I brushed it back with my manicured hand. I finished peeing, wiped myself, flushed, and pulled up my panties. As I walked to the sink, I observed her watching me.

"Fuck." I couldn't believe what I had become.

I descended into depression beyond suffering. The thought of death felt more like the possibility of liberation. My cavern was dark with rare, contaminated air – a big vacuum where life did not happen. The light in the room bothered me. The air burned my nostrils. Life became a chore and a drag.

*

I RECEIVED AN EMAIL from Zoë – brief – addressed to all her friends in her mailing list: "*The doctor found a tumor in my uterus. I am going for more testing to find out if it is malignant. Cross your fingers. I'll keep you posted.*"

The next day when the phone rang, I took the receiver and heard Zoë's voice shaking. I covered my mouth with my free hand when I heard her say, "Lisbeth, I have stage four uterine cancer."

Jussef was snapping random pictures around the house. He took a photo of me in that precise moment. In the picture, I am sitting on the bed looking through a window.

"What did you say?" I asked her.

"What happened?" Jussef asked. I motioned for him to wait.

"I am angry," she said. "I do check ups every six months. I had bleeding going on for two years and a belly as if I was five months pregnant. The doctor kept saying it was normal. And now she tells me, it's stage four."

"Oh, Zoë. There must be a mistake." I tried to reassure her. "What are you going to do next?"

"I'm going for an emergency surgery tomorrow, and then we'll figure out a plan of action. I'll let you know of any news. Lisa Harrison will be in contact with you. Remember my friend, Lisa?"

"Of course, Zoë. She used to live with you on 98th Street, didn't she?"

"Yes. Her. She will call you to let you know how the surgery went."

"I wish you the best of luck. I will be thinking of you with all my heart." I told her. I put the phone down.

"What's wrong? What happened?" Jussef asked me as I burst out crying.

"Zoë has cancer, and it's at stage four."

"Coño," he said, "Lisbeth, lo siento mucho."

He hugged me and held me silently as I sobbed on his shoulder.

"Let's wish for the best," he said.

Lisa called the next day to say that the surgery had removed most of the tumor, but there was a bit left in the liver because they couldn't reach it. Zoë took the first round of chemo with stoicism. We bombarded her with well wishes, books, and articles we thought might help. Zoë replied to my contribution with an angry email.

> I can't live one day without people reminding me that I have cancer. I feel well; I don't have pain or feel anything except for the fact that they gave me the diagnosis of a terminally ill person. Would you and everybody else please stop sending presents and reminders of my cancer?

I wrote back.

Why is it you with cancer when it is me who doesn't want to live?

Then, I discarded the message. She needed optimism and laughter, and I wasn't fit to give any.

"I want to be there with you," I said over the phone.

"What are you going to do, yell at the doctors?" she replied. Again, after I hung up the phone, the best answers came to me.

> I'd hug you! If you don't feel like speaking, I'd sit by your bed, hold your hand, and share the wisdom of silence with you. I'd hang a nice chime in your room. If you don't want to smell flowers, I'd ask all your beloved friends' children to paint

> flowers for you, and I'd paste them all over your room to bring smiles to your face. I'd dress up as a clown and be silly for you. I will never allow you to see a doctor by yourself again. There has to be several extra people with you, all of them taking notes and asking questions.

But I never did. I was too far away when my friend most needed me. I didn't have any practical contribution to make, except to keep sending my love and support.

Zoë approached her cancer like a project – moving through a list of responsibilities to complete. She continued working as a counselor and made legal arrangements so that her daughter, who was then eight, would never need to worry. She sued the doctor who had treated her for a number of years for failing to run the tests that would have made an early diagnosis possible. She tried every available treatment and volunteered for clinical trials in a desperate effort to stop the cancer.

"What is the prognosis?" I asked.

"There won't be any positive outcome, Lisbeth. I am just prolonging my life. I want to give all I can to my daughter."

I took to card making. Each card was a special creation for my friend. The hours I spent in those small drawings, paintings, and collages were my special prayers for her health. I visualized cancer as a weed growing in her body, slowly taking over her organs and cells, feeding from them. Then I transformed that image into a colorful vine, engulfing the weed, sprouting inside of her, bringing new healthy cells to her body. With every stroke of my colored pencils, I repeated, "May you be healthy again. May you overcome this and live a long life."

I put the cards in small packets with herbs and vegetables from my garden, my offering of anti-oxidants to battle the cancer. She welcomed them with joy and encouragement.

"You should do this for business, Lisbeth. The cards are great. The nurses and my friends love them. Why don't you sell them?" she asked during a call from her hospital bed.

For a while, it seemed that her efforts were working. She made plans to move to the Caribbean, but when she understood that death was imminent, she changed course, sold most of her property, and moved from the Manhattan neighborhood she had lived for 25 years to Riverdale in the Bronx. She resettled near the best school she could possibly find, where she could trust her daughter's education would be taken care of from that point to the end of high school. She also hired a nanny to look after the child in case she went too soon. When everything had been decided and set in place, Zoë took a road trip to say goodbye to her dear friends in California, Oregon, and Oklahoma.

New hair had started to grow in her head. It came back curly and darker. She looked cute in her housedress and sneakers. We hugged when she stepped out of her car in our driveway.

"I didn't know your house was so big," she said. "It's like a mansion by New York standards."

"We'll need walkie-talkies to talk from room to room," her daughter joked.

It didn't take her long to notice the tension between Jussef and me, and she soon began interrogating me. I explained that I was tied up in immigration limbo without documents and couldn't proceed with any aspect of my life. I couldn't work or go to college; I couldn't even get a divorce without fear of losing my son.

"Why do you want to go back to school?" she asked.

"There is a Masters in Education program I can do at The University Learning Center in town, but I don't have any money under my name, and I can't ask for a loan because I don't have a social security number. Jussef's salary disqualified me for scholarships."

"Did you ask him for money?"

"Yes, but he said we didn't have money for that. I feel trapped."

"If money is all you need, that's easy to solve." She then directed me to turn on the computer and right there, she signed up for credit and offered herself as my guarantor. "It's done," she said. "Get the Master's and as soon as you find a job, pay the credit. It's in my name. I know you won't disgrace it."

We went to a rodeo together and ate funnel cake. She invited us to the hotel swimming pool, where we watched the kids play and ogled the hot cowboys in town for the rodeo.

"I like that," she said pointing her chin in the direction of a tall man with horse chaps over his jeans and spurs on the back of his boots.

"Like an egg in a frying pan," I said.

"How is that?" she giggled.

I made a sizzling sound with my teeth, and we both cracked up laughing.

We visited the buffalo herd in the Tall Grass Prairie Reserve in Pawhuska and the Pioneer Woman monument in Ponca City. Back at the house, we took pictures sitting at the bench in my front lawn, framed by the blooming redbud and the flowerpots. Ramón had come to visit with his college sweetheart, who joined us on the bench. Saul and Kathy climbed on the tree while we chatted and enjoyed our beautiful and rare time together.

*

THANKS TO ZOË'S name on the credit line, I entered graduate school. I knew that most of my obsessions derived from the fact that I didn't have an intellectual outlet to anchor me in reality. Graduate school served exactly that purpose. I spent the next year and a half reading, writing papers, and taking tests. I also had a new space where I met people, even if through Interactive Television, one form of distance education that uses a closed circuit of television connecting universities with remote locations. Now, my mind was busy with issues other than groceries and afterschool activities. I continued advocating for Jussef to pay an immigration lawyer to get green cards for the family. This would allow me to work.

The green cards arrived shortly before I finished graduate school in December 2006. This time I wore a cap and gown despite the sixty plus pounds I carried and took pictures with my husband and children. My sheltered life was complete. I had everything I had wished for: a family, two healthy children, a house, and a solid education. We were not rich, but we enjoyed a comfortable middle-class life that included great health insurance and long vacations, two luxuries not many people could afford.

*

"DR. SMITH I sent you a letter two weeks ago and wondered if you had any time to consider my request?" I asked when I ran into the President of the Northern Oklahoma College in Tonkawa, Oklahoma.

The college had recruited me to run the language program I had designed as a graduate student. I worked for 60 hours a week for the next six months, teaching Spanish to first responders and business people in this small town of wheat farmers. I also taught ESL to manufacturing workers. I developed these classes and their marketing campaign on a small stipend.

I had sent a letter to the college president summarizing what I had done and what I could do next to contribute to the program's success. In it, I asked for a paid position.

"Oh, yes, Mrs. Coiman. Can you remind me again?" Dr. Smith asked as he kept walking.

"I'm sorry. You must be on your way somewhere. It's just that I have tried to talk to you and you have not been available." I explained to him that I had worked really hard for the program and expected at this point to have a paid position.

"I did read your letter," he finally admitted.

"Do you have an answer for me?" I asked. I waited for his response under the shade of the tree near the administration building. Despite the sweltering heat, I smiled.

"The answer is we don't have a position for you, Mrs. Coiman. You became too aggressive, too soon."

"I understand, sir. It's been a pleasure working for you," I said as I stretched my hand out to him. If asking for a decent pay after working 60 hours a week for six months meant aggressiveness, I didn't want to work for that employer.

I turned on my heels and ran back to my office crying. It took me an hour and a half to pack my teaching materials. I had put the best of me into this project. I had bought all I had needed with my own money. I left in anger.

*

IT WAS THE BEGINNING of summer 2007, and I was 43 years old. I felt used and doomed. I had permanent residence now and was free to work, but jobs were few in an oil-refining town. Life lacked importance. Suicide became my macabre thought. I thought about it, and then fantasized about it, imagining scenarios of how people I loved reacting to news of my death.

Jussef planned a trip to Venezuela. I refused to join him. It was too much hassle to see people I loathed.

"I will go only if I can stay away from our mothers," I told him.

"You know my mother will be offended if you are in Caracas and don't visit her."

"I don't care if she is offended. I won't go if it is a requirement," I said.

In the end, he took Saul with him, and I remained alone. Ramón had finished college and was in another state doing his internship. I used my time to plan my suicide.

It was a Saturday morning. I sat in the recliner on the back patio across from the maple tree. I had a bottle of wine, a tall glass, and a sharpened knife on the table. I called Venezuela first to hear Saul's voice as a way of saying goodbye, before cutting my veins to bleed in the summer heat. As soon as I put the phone down, it rang. It was Ramón. He was in Colorado, but his lease in Oklahoma had expired. He needed help moving out.

"Mom, please can you go to my apartment in Norman and move me out? Also, can you keep my stuff for a couple of months while I finish my internship?" he asked.

I got up from the chair, crossed the street, and borrowed my neighbor's pick-up. Norman - the college town where the University of Oklahoma is located - was a good two and half hours away from Ponca City. I cautiously drove the distance in three hours, as I was using a borrowed vehicle. His college friends were there to help me pack and load Ramón's belongings into the truck, but not everything fit. I promised to come back the next day for the rest. I returned the pick-up to my neighbor and went to sleep.

Suicide could wait a day or two. Ramón needed me.

Sunday, I got up around ten, ate breakfast, and started driving. When I passed the 15 miles marker going southbound on the I-35 to Norman, a white pick-up about 1000 feet ahead of me, driving northbound, veered off its lane into the opposing traffic. It struck an SUV, sending it flying into the air. The SUV landed head first in a ditch past the shoulder on the right. Cars collided and skidded in the aftermath. I drove to the shoulder and called 911. After signaling to the incoming traffic to slow down, I walked to the scene. The SUV was in flames. Somebody rushed toward it with a fire extinguisher. I saw the disfigured bodies of two men in the front seat of the SUV. Liquid poured from their heads. The occupants had died on impact. I called 911 again. Others tended to the driver of the white pick-up.

"Anybody speak Spanish here?" someone yelled.

"I do," I said.

"Please, take care of the woman in the center lane."

We were in the plains on a sunny Sunday at 100 F degrees. Tall grass bordered the I-35 on both sides. I walked to the median, a patch of grass large enough to contain two vehicles side by side. There I met a woman with intense black eyes trying to run to the crashed SUV. "¿Cómo se llama Usted, señora?" I asked.

"María. Yo quiero ir para el otro lado a ver a mi esposo. ¿Por qué nadie lo está ayudando?" she asked.

"Your husband is in a better place now," I said. The fact didn't register, so she asked again why nobody was rushing to help her husband like they were rushing to help the occupants of the other vehicle.

They were migrant workers, roofers driving from Nebraska to Texas for work. Her husband had been driving ahead of the rest of the family with his friend. The woman followed behind with their daughter and her brother-in-law.

"We just stopped about a mile ago, and he blessed the girl. He's a good father. Ayúdelo, por favor."

I looked at the disoriented girl, a rag doll without anyone to hold her tight, her mother sobbing and screaming, and her uncle like a toy robot going around in circles with his hands over his head, raising his eyes now and again to the bright sky. I thought about my son, Saul, and what I had been about to do before Ramón's call. I had planned to leave my child too, as a rag doll, without anything to hold onto.

I spent three hours on that highway in the scorching Oklahoma heat with a child who had just lost her father and a woman who had just lost the man she loved. I helped them communicate with the first responders that had been my students only a month before. I couldn't do this to my sons. Never.

*

WHEN JAY LENO'S jokes about Britney Spears' erratic behavior rocked the *Tonight Show* audience, I experienced a brief psychotic episode and cried at every punch line. His entire twelve-minute stand-up monologue was delivered to me, from the inside of the TV, looking directly into my eyes. Jay spoke to me and about me. For liability purposes, he used Britney Spears' name, but for all I knew, I was the joke.

Sitting on the sofa in front of the TV with my legs curled up to my chest, I wept bitterly. Jussef looked at me, unable to understand how a funny show could affect me so much. With the rest of the sanity I held, I summoned the strength to call my doctor and report that Jay Leno was making fun of me. The doctor adjusted my medication, which placed me again on the road to recovery. That's how I first understood how to separate the creations in my mind from reality.

From then on, I used the famous comedian's monologue as my indicator for psychosis. If Leno was talking about me, I had to call my doctor. I thought of Leno as an old friend who inspired trust. The decision to call the doctor was born from some anchor in reality that allowed me to see the absurdity of this. If my husband or children had asked me to call my doctor, it wouldn't have worked in the same way. My family is my support network; I trust them with my life, but I couldn't depend on them to recognize my symptoms or make treatment decisions. My recovery stood on self-realization and independence, on the development of idiosyncratic coping skills that helped me deal with thoughts and emotions that were far beyond rational comprehension.

The crises continued, but episodes were less intense and the recovery time shorter. It helped that I could recognize my symptoms from the start—speeding thoughts, speech problems, obsessions, and Jay Leno. From time to time, I heard the voice in my head calling me by my second name, Carolina. It was an authoritarian voice that sounded like a reprimand. Occasionally, I saw cockroaches crawling diagonally on the bathroom wall.

Depression usually started with agitation. Alone at home, after Jussef and the kids were gone for the day, I'd pace aimlessly inside the house, unable to make small decisions: Should I fix breakfast or make the bed first? Frustrated, I'd cry for a while and then drag my feet for the rest of the day. It wasn't the depression of TV commercial standards. Sure, I cried a lot, but it was always from agitation, which came with a significant amount of self-derogatory language.

I created tools to deal with each of my symptoms. I wrote a cue card for each day of the week telling me what to do. Mondays: change sheets and clean bathrooms. Tuesdays: sweep, mop, and vacuum. And so on. When I woke up disoriented and noticed the aimless pacing, I retrieved my cue cards from a recipe box on the kitchen counter and followed the instructions I had written for myself.

Crocheting became the antidote to obsessions and speeding thoughts. My mother was an avid crochetter. She could fabricate laced tablecloths and blankets, doilies, and baby clothes in the most elaborate of stiches. Always careful to stay away from her beatings, I deliberately avoided learning any craft from her, but isolation changes you. I bought crochet books and magazines and taught myself my mother's favorite craft and pastime. Crocheting requires a great deal of counting, repeating patterns, focus, and patience. My mind was unable to hold a thought, but I could count to ten repeatedly.

When the pain of the memories from my childhood became unbearable and the voice in my head called my name or insulted me, I took to gardening. The repetitive movement of weeding dandelions on my knees, or cutting the dead heads of flowers, or digging in the dirt to plant new seeds soothed my pain like a balm. I let the voice speak without trying to silence it or deny it. When I listened carefully, I identified it as the voice of my mother who never had a nice word for me. I pitied her luck to be locked in my head for the rest of my days without access to my life.

Hamsa Hand

LOUSY JOB AFTER lousy job followed, but I held onto my life with a firm grip. I worked briefly as the Executive Director of a Salvation Army shelter in Ponca City, and learned about the scores of mentally ill people who are homeless. I thought that one day it could be me, so I set a deadline for paying off our mortgage. I opened an IRA account and set out to contribute the maximum allowable amount per year. If everything else failed, I'd have a roof over my head. I didn't use one single penny for shoes or jewelry. I needed to catch up with life.

During spring break 2009, I took Saul with me to New York to visit Zoë. I knew the end was near, and I wanted to see her, and tell her how much I loved her and how grateful I was for her friendship. Zoë had been sick for five years. She had done everything money and prayer could make possible to prolong her life and earn a few more years to watch her child grow. She endured the invasive treatment without complaint or self-pity.

The colorful head cover and tattooed eyebrows couldn't hide the fact that Zoë no longer had hair on her body. Rounds of chemotherapy had left her with greenish skin. She continued to give advice and generous praise in her weak voice. She couldn't hold a dish or cut a tomato but insisted on cooking breakfast for us. She put two eggs in a skillet. As she tried to flip them, the eggs fell on the floor. I rushed to help and saw that the palms of her hands were almost burned from the chemo.

We talked about Ramón and how he had become a good man in spite of me – all he went through when I was a single mother and during each of my breakdowns. We enjoyed watching our children play together, those who had been born only three weeks apart.

"You are so brave," I said. "The most daring thing I've done in years is this job at the Salvation Army. Here you are, five years of cancer treatment. I really admire you." My troubles seemed so small compared to her battle.

"You have to live your life now. You don't know when is it going to be taken away from you. Stop complaining about being mentally ill, about living in the middle of nowhere," she commanded with a mother's tone. "This is the life you have." She continued talking and arranging things around her house, fluffing pillows, pushing chairs under the table. I followed her as she counseled in her direct and honest way.

"Jussef has his issues," she said, "and we know his mother is a black cloud over your home, but he has been a good thing in your life. I think he deserves you giving that relationship a second chance. He has weathered the storm with you in your most difficult moments, and he is now astray, but what are you doing to recover your wit and charm, or to be his friend, or fall in love with your partner again? You are comfortable in your resentment because it doesn't require an effort on your part. Marriage is a two-way street, Lisbeth." She used a disciplinarian tone, and I didn't have the heart or right to argue with her.

That night, we played Rock Band with the children on the top floor of her three-story Victorian house. It was an expansive space with a TV set, a sofa, a spare bed for visitors, and a bathroom. While the children played the drums and the guitar, Zoë and I sang the vocals. We rocked at the edge of the sofa.

She held the mic in her hands, and I leaned my head towards hers. We smiled at my out-of-tune shrills, while poorly interpreting the classic, "*Livin' on a Prayer.*" We held each other tight, saved the tears, and gave all the love of a friendship that transcended illness. When we said goodnight, we hugged silently, and we didn't dare let words betray our strength. I held her scent and warmth. Her child and husband stood nearby watching another farewell.

"Goodbye, my friend. I love you," she said.

"I love you too, Zoë."

"Stay strong," she whispered.

I continued to write letters and stored them in a small box.

*

AFTER TEACHING ALL day at East Central High School in Tulsa, where I had worked for the last few months, I started my long commute back to Ponca City. The two-hour drive through the endless plains gave me enough time to cool down before meeting Jussef and the boys for dinner. Through the windshield, I saw the cows grazing against the display of reds, purple, and blue hues, and the clouds above about to burst into a dramatic weather event.

On Highway 412, I thought of my third period ESL class—26 students speaking six languages and adjusting to their new homeland. When the bell rang after lunch, I stood at the classroom door, greeting each student with a handshake. I was able to tell who had taken something during the break by the way their hands trembled. Sometimes, I could smell weed coming from the bathroom. "Maestra, you can buy even Pepto-Bismol in that bathroom. They have a pharmacy there," a student in my sixth period Spanish class told me once.

And this is how work was – a series of disappointments and secrets up and down the halls. A clear division between the faculty and the administration kept the air toxic inside the Art Deco building, but as a new first year teacher, I didn't have any alliances. Although hired to teach ESL, I taught two additional crowded Spanish classes and translated during parent-teacher conferences.

Back in Ponca City, my weekends were mostly spent preparing classes and grading papers. I had stitched myself into a quilt of complications that started with a long commute. My youngest was in eighth grade, and we learned that he needed more attention and a strong parental presence to keep him on track. My work buried my schedule. I felt I had abandoned him. I stopped eating and often cried for leaving my son behind for a dead-end job, for the poor decisions that got me there, and for Zoë.

I struggled with sleep and decided I needed to move to Owasso, a town north of Tulsa, because I was unable to drive anymore. The company Jussef worked for closed its research center in Ponca City and relocated most of its employees to nearby Bartlesville. Instead of moving to another oil town, we decided to wait until Saul finished the semester to buy a house in Owasso because we needed a good school district for him. Owasso was a good middle point between Jussef's new location and my job.

*

THE CLINKING OF KEYS began to annoy me. I walked to a student's desk and looked at the macramé key ring he was playing with. My eyes fixed on the thing, and I was suddenly in the house I grew up with my mother standing over me. She was holding a multicolor macramé whip and accusing me of laziness. She raised the whip-holding hand well above her head and let it fall on my arm with all her strength.

She had come back from work, showing off the new whip she had commissioned. I hated its maker, and I would have killed them had I known who had made such a horrific tool to punish us. She didn't have a real excuse to punish me, except that she wanted to break it in. I extended my arms out to try to block the blows, but she moved rapidly to my legs, and then to my back as I pleaded with her to stop.

"No, please no! I won't do it anymore!" I screamed. Beatings always ended with me promising not to do something I had never done in the first place.

When she was finished, she said, "Ta' bien bueno." In my room, I sobbed on my bed while I touched the knots on my arms and legs.

I looked at my student, horrified. "Put it away please. It's annoying." I placed my left hand on my right shoulder and tried unsuccessfully to massage the pain. I felt knots on my arms and my shoulder pulling my neck. Luckily, the bell was about to ring. After assigning homework and dismissing the students, I turned to the wall and cried, drying my tears with the back of my chalk-covered hand. I turned off the light, closed the classroom door behind me, and delighted in the idea that I could roll down the window, open my hand, and release my terror to the glorious sunset on my drive back home through The Plains.

*

"I'M MOVING INTO hospice care. I am scared." Zoë's words were punctuated by a weak cough

Tears flooded my eyes, and I pulled over to stop on the shoulder. The strong thrash of the rough pavement under the tires startled me for a second. "I want to be with you," I said.

"No, Lisbeth. My friend, Generose, is taking care of me. She will be with me until the last moment. I just wanted to say goodbye to you and say I love you." Her voice was barely audible.

"Promise me you will always leave the door open for my child. If you find it closed, kick it open," she said, taking time to breathe.

"I will," I replied, choking down my tears.

"Promise me you will always live your best life," she said in a whisper.

That was the last time I heard Zoë's voice. I cried in the car. It took me a while to pull myself together and restart my long drive home. Night had already darkened when I arrived. I hugged Jussef and cried again. I feared that by letting go of Zoë I would be forever swept into the dark hole of my past and its somber mood.

*

SHORTLY AFTER ZOË'S last phone call, I received a small greeting card in the mail. It was fall.

> *Good luck, happiness, hope, fun, money, health, joy, pleasure, friendship and satisfaction. I hope this is what you've been looking for. Love, Zoë*

Those were her last wishes for me. I detached a tiny light blue velvet bag stapled to the card. Inside, there was an inch and a half long hamsa of delicate silver wire curled into a fine filigree work. I placed it in my hand and closed my fingers over the fine piece of jewelry. I felt Zoë's hand in the pendant. She held my hand for the last time, and I squeezed it tight.

I understood it was Zoë's way of saying goodbye and saying she would continue to protect me from wherever she was going next. I had told her about my first hamsa and how just after I had received it, I met her and then Jussef, the two people who turned my life around. I also told her I had lost the hamsa and was always looking to replace it. I never thought she had paid attention to my tale of magic and love. I held it again as I wiped my tears. So many years later, she told me she had heard every word.

Veterans Day

ZOË DIED ON Saul's thirteenth birthday.

During the months between her last call and Veterans Day, her friend Lisa Harrison kept all of Zoë's friends and relatives informed through regular emails titled, "Health Updates," which let us know when Zoë had been moved from hospice care at home to hospice care at the hospital, and what kind of care she had decided to receive in her last days.

Lisa called me at work. I was in the middle of my Spanish class when the phone rang. I picked up and heard her voice. "Lisbeth? This is Lisa Harrison. Zoë just passed away in her sleep."

I excused myself from the 48 rioting students in front of me and sat silently on my desk for a few minutes. They screamed at each other, left the classroom without permission, and wrecked the room while I stood by the chalkboard with a vacant look in my eyes. The bell finally rang.

I feared a downward spiral into madness. I didn't want the hate and resentment I felt from losing Zoë to take control of me, transforming me into a bitter and withdrawn woman. For the first time in the twenty-five years since meeting Zoë, I had to hold onto myself.

I went to work in a haze of medication, robotic and unable to control my students. To get through the days, I used her words as my mantra: "Live your best life now. You don't know when is it going to be taken away from you." But I wasn't living. Instead, I worked myself numb, not leaving school until 10 at night, eating instant ramen for dinner when I got home, and inducing slumber with medication. It was an artificial existence, but it kept me going until my family moved to Owasso with me in December.

*

WHEN IT WAS TIME to attend her memorial, I drove to the Tulsa airport to take a plane to La Guardia, where I met Ramón. The chill January air hit us when we stepped out of the subway looking for our hotel, a cute boutique lodging somewhere on Broadway. We checked ourselves into a double room and headed out immediately in search of food. We hadn't had a meaningful conversation in a while, and now sitting in a restaurant in NYC with Ramón felt like a great luxury and accomplishment. He told me about his life as an independent adult. I lifted the spoon to my mouth and smiled, looking at his intense eyes. He made me so proud.

I had come to NYC several times since 1989, always to meet Zoë. This time was no different. The next day, we walked the cold and busy streets of upper Manhattan to the synagogue where Zoë's memorial service was taking place. When we entered, the auditorium buzzed with people mostly in their late fifties and sixties, but also some teenagers around Zoë's daughter's age. I scanned the room from left to right trying to identify anybody I knew. Zoë's closest friends were in that room hugging and crying on each other's shoulders and re-telling common anecdotes, but I was anonymous to all but a handful of them.

I sat in the auditorium with my son and nearly 200 other guests, drying my tears with Kleenex. It felt awfully strange to be in the audience, as if I were about to listen to a concert when my heart ached from the loss of my dear friend. Even though I had had plenty of time to prepare for her death, the grief was still raw and painful. Zoë had planned for us to celebrate her life instead of mourning her passing. That sentiment was present during the entire event, where laughter mixed with tears as the speakers took turns on the stage.

The female minister who performed her wedding service in 2004 opened the memorial. She praised Zoë's stoicism and her will to live. Then a man played the guitar and sang a song that he and Zoë had performed together during her time at the theater company. Several others took to the stage in costumes from one of the play from the children's theater to perform a segment of their most successful piece. I remembered having seen a picture of Zoë in a similar outfit some twenty years ago, when she wrote about the children's play *Bushwacked.* Most of the attendants laughed and sang along to the familiar tunes, but it all seemed foreign and distant to me.

Through her siblings, I learned about how as a teenager, Zoë had convinced them to climb on a boat for what would be an afternoon of fun. They all ended up on an island off the coast of the US. We cried and laughed with the memories of her wit and youthful personality. Generose took the mic to tell us about how Zoë had provided a home for her when she was a single mother attending college. Lisa spoke last, reminding us that Zoë's constant advice could drive anyone crazy.

In the center of the auditorium, to my left, Kathy grieved the death of her mother, surrounded by a group of teenagers, friends and cousins, who comforted her whenever she cried. She was at the center of this great network of friends Zoë had created to ensure the girl would never be alone. I was sure Zoë had made each one of us promise we would never lose sight of the child, that we would always know if she was okay.

At the reception, I looked for Kathy and Zoë's husband, Rob, to express my condolences and say goodbye. I approached Rob standing near the hors d'oeuvres table. He was putting something in his mouth when I got close to him. He gave me a cold side hug. I didn't see Crystal, the girl's loving nanny. Kathy accepted my condolences politely and moved on quickly back to her group.

I found Ellie next. "I want to keep in touch," I said. We exchanged phone numbers and reminisced about when had we met in Venezuela all those years ago.

"There is a bench in Central Park with Zoë's name. I encourage you to go there before you leave town," Ellie said before moving across the room to talk to somebody else.

When I spotted Lisa, I cried. "Thanks for inviting me, and thank you for sending me all those health updates. I'm so sorry I couldn't be here when it happened," I said.

"There wasn't much you could do anyway, Lisbeth. Don't worry about that."

"How is Luke?" I always wanted to know about "Zoë's children." Lisa pointed out her son in the crowd, and I marveled at how much he had grown.

"Can you please introduce me to Generose?" I asked her. I was anxious to meet the woman who had cared for Zoë in her final moments.

We looked for Generose in the room, and Lisa introduced us. Generose and I hugged, united by the common gratitude to our late friend.

"Thank you for taking care of Zoë in her final moments," I said.

"You don't need to thank me."

"I wanted to be here so badly, but I couldn't."

After this brief exchange, I lingered around the snacks, making small talk here and there, answering the question, "How did you meet Zoë?" It was obvious I was not part of the main group. Her memorial had turned out like a high school reunion, fun and celebratory, nothing to feel sad about, just like she wanted. About half an hour later, Ramón and I left.

As we left the synagogue and walked through the cold streets of Manhattan to Central Park, my son and I marveled at the life of Zoë, the most extraordinary woman we would ever know. We talked about what she had given us, and how we would always miss her. Her dedication to improve our lives and her stoic fight against cancer will always be an inspiration for us. We strolled in Central Park for the rest of the day, looking for the Zoë's bench without any other reference than the sketchy directions Ellie had given us. We didn't find it, but we sat in silence on a bench somewhere near Bethesda Terrace and thought about her.

"Time to go back," I said after a while in silence. And we rushed back to the hotel and then to LaGuardia to catch our respective planes back home.

*

GRIEVING AND EXHAUSTED from the trip, I still made it on time to my over packed Spanish class on Monday. Though I was determined to complete my first year of teaching in America and to complete all the requirements for certification, I knew some things had to change. I decided to talk to the principal about the classroom conditions. I had to be assertive and strong as a nail.

My feet ached most of the time, and a chalk-caused allergy blurred my vision. I felt an urgent need to tackle this new problem head-on. On a piece of paper, I wrote down my issues and the action I needed and expected: reduced class sizes or help with crowd control. Between classes, I stood in front of the chalkboard and practiced my speech to the principal looking briefly at the cheat-sheet in my hand.

When I felt confident, I collected my things and grabbed my piece of paper with three bullet points decorated with two arrows, bold red handwriting, and underlining for urgency. I headed for the bathroom and, at the toilet, I felt the long, almost orgasmic relief of my bladder draining. While I sat, I repeated my opening line.

Downstairs, a student in detention cursed at the teacher on duty. The phone rang unattended. I entered the office and pretended to be invisible when I passed by the adults sitting in the waiting area. I knocked shyly at Mrs. Hugging's door and waited to be called in.

"Come in, Mrs. Coiman. How can I help you today?" Mrs. Huggins asked with a smile on her face.

"I need a mental health break," I said.

Mrs. Huggins, who was not smiling anymore, put up a shield, as if she suddenly felt the need to defend herself. "You never said you were disabled."

"Because I am not. I am a perfectly able individual, but the conditions in my classroom and this school, in general, are not healthy. Anybody would go crazy here. There are rumors about my sexuality. I have to break up fights. I have at least eight students with special needs that I am teaching without an assistant. Absenteeism and tardiness are rampant. Name a cause of disruption, and I bet it happens in my Spanish class because it is too big, forty-eight students too big to be exact. The class is unmanageable." I looked at the paper in my hand but didn't read the words anymore.

"Go ahead," Mrs. Huggins said with a smirk.

"I am mentally ill, but don't worry," I said before Mrs. Huggins had time to interrupt. "I'm under the care of professionals, and I take my medications as indicated. But I fear this situation could spin out of control. That's why I need a break. Can you split the class?"

"We don't have another teacher for that."

"And you also think I'm coping well because the students haven't seen me crying yet, but let me tell you something, Mrs. Huggins, I'm not coping well.

You need to split the class in two, even if it means hiring another teacher." I felt proud of myself for telling Mrs. Huggins how it was.

"Don't get ahead of yourself. I can't hire another teacher," she said.

"Then, how are you going to help me manage forty-eight students in one class and forty in the other? In third period, one guy sells pot in my classroom, and I think he must be snorting something because he bounces off the walls and has a pale sweat. That is not normal, Mrs. Huggins. I need to know how you are going to help me." My voice was firm, but my eyes welled up fast.

Mrs. Huggins stood up from her chair and extended her hand to me. "That's for you to figure out, Mrs. Coiman. Don't put up with unacceptable behavior, and send any student who is giving you grief directly to me."

"I see. Good afternoon, Mrs. Huggins. Thanks for listening," I said as I lifted myself from the chair. I put the piece of paper with my three points in my bag, grabbed the doorknob, cold and sleek in my hand, and left the office swiftly.

I completed the school year successfully but was grateful when a district contract with Teach for America took my job away. It took me until the middle of summer to think of a plan for myself.

My psychiatrist asked me one day, "How are you going to honor Zoë's legacy?"

"I have to live my best life. I have to come to terms with my past and give the best I can in what I most love to do."

"What is it that you love doing?" he asked.

"Writing and gardening," I said.

Garden Therapy

BY THE FALL I had found job as a school district interpreter and translator. It was the lowest paying position I ever had, but the perfect job for me. It suited my personality and condition. It was intellectually engaging and free of conflict and major stressors.

One Saturday morning in 2010, I opened the mailbox by the curb and stood in shock. There was a letter in the mail from Zoë. I couldn't understand. My mind resisted logical explanations. This must be a very cruel joke. I opened the envelope to find a check for five thousand dollars. I cried, still unable to understand, overwhelmed as I was by emotion. I called Rob.

"Rob, this is Lisbeth," I said.

"What's up, Lis?" When the familiar voice with New York accent answered the phone, I stiffened.

"Oh, nothing. It's just that I got this letter in the mail. I don't understand, Rob. There is a check from Zoë," I said.

"Yes, Lisbeth. She left some money for you," he explained.

"What?"

"She did. You were mentioned in her will, but because you are not a citizen, her estate decided to send you a check for this amount, so you don't have to pay taxes."

“I’m in shock,” I said after I took a moment to recover.

“Enjoy,” he said before hanging up.

I showed everybody my check. I wanted to tell the world what she had done for me. I used the money for a down payment on my first car.

A few weekends later, I took a gram of gold my former boss at the Caracas Hilton had given me and Zoë's hamsa to a jeweler in Tulsa. I asked him to melt the gold to bathe the hamsa in it.

He was doubtful. "Why would you like to do that? This is pure gold."

"Because it was the last present my dearest friend gave me," I answered.

"You must've loved that friend a lot," he said.

“I still love her.”

I continued to improve my writing and translation skills and earned a reputation as a fast and diligent worker, but soon the district placed me in another dysfunctional position. This time, I was supposed to be a travelling teacher serving four schools while keeping my interpreting and translating duties.

I started my day at the high school. There I clocked in, checked my mail, updated my planner, took out one folder for each of the schools I visited during the day, and then walked along a wooded outdoor path to the nearby eighth grade center. Then I dragged my feet for the next three hours. The students didn’t cooperate. They saw an ESL teacher as the person who made them work and didn’t help doing homework. The teaching assistants were no better. They saw me more as a threat to their employment than as a teacher serving ESL students.

I advocated for the ESL students and worked on modifications of objectives and assignments to help the ESL students meet standards. I tried to work with the teachers, but modification to them meant my sitting next to the students and whispering the answers to questions that were way above the students' skills.

The principal saw me as the obstacle bringing her good numbers down. Traditionally numbers had been up, thanks to the diligent help of teaching assistants whispering answers to students. The rest of the faculty didn't know if I was a teacher, an assistant, or an ESL coordinator. I didn't have a desk to sit at the school, and the misinformation, bickering and dysfunctionality at the eighth grade center made teaching almost impossible and me miserable.

Additionally, I had to walk back to the high school and drive to the sixth grade center to teach a couple of times a week for one hour to a small group of middle grade scholars. From the sixth grade center, I drove a few blocks to the ninth grade center for my midday monitoring of advanced ESL students. The best principal of the district, another Huggins, always met me with a smile, supporting me in my efforts. The afternoon belonged to the high school, where I barely found enough time to gulp down lunch. The teaching assistant at the high school comforted me and encouraged me to continue my good work. If needed, the high school principal provided support, and observations that were more than satisfactory.

One day, by mistake, I took the flash drive with the only digital copy of my memoir, along with some short stories, and lesson plans from the year before to school with me. As I left the eighth grade center to go to the sixth grade center, I realized I had left the flash drive in the computer I was using. I made a mental note to pick it up the next day because I was running late.

The next day, as I was entering the eighth grade center, through the back door, I heard a voice over the loud speaker. "Somebody left a purple flash drive yesterday. It is now in the lost and found box. Please come to pick it up," said the principal.

I checked the lost and found, but it wasn't mine. When I went back to the computer, I found it wasn't there either. I asked the janitor and the students if they had seen it. I tore my high school classroom upside down, but I never found the flash drive. I was devastated.

The thought that the grade eighth grade principal had found the flash drive and thus discovered the content of my book, where I spoke about my mental condition, mortified me to the point where I couldn't sleep. Repetitive thoughts so characteristic of my obsessions played like a broken record in my mind. Stress increased. On Sunday, the headline of the Art Section of the Tulsa World displayed the working title of my book, "The Shattered Mirror." Paranoia sank in again. Back at school on Monday, I felt all the loudspeaker messages were directed at me. I had to call my doctor to increase the medication once more. I couldn't hide my contempt for the eighth grade center and the principal anymore. She became the worse bully I have ever seen in a school.

"I am here to do an observation," the eighth grade principal said when she dropped by unannounced in my classroom.

"I have been observed twice already, once by the ninth grade center and once by the high school. How many observations are there supposed to be?" I asked.

I wondered if it was even legal. Was it normal for a teacher to report to and be observed by four principals at three different schools? No other teacher in the district had to undergo this level of scrutiny.

"You didn't do very well in the observation, Mrs. Coiman. I noticed you don't have much patience with your students. You don't smile at all. And I think you should increase your niceties with the teaching assistants." Her words came at me as if through a tube, delayed and cold.

I felt abused, but tried to keep my head down and continue travelling from one school to another. Finally, I couldn't take it anymore; stress took the best of me. I recorded one of those meetings with the principal.

"Use that smile of yours, Mrs. Coiman," she said. "Your students are afraid of you. Do you know why?"

"I don't have any idea," I said, looking past her face through the window to the bright day outside. But I knew. The toxic environment and rumors had escalated, and now the principal was drilling me on it. "*Will I ever be able to find a normal job?*" I asked myself while the principal noted the strokes I made with my pencil as a possible sign of anger.

I had to prove that she was a bully. I brought the small recorder to my department meeting and asked my colleagues for advice on what to do. Somebody from that meeting told the eighth grade principal, who then moved heaven and earth to kick me out of the district. I was happy to go by June 2012.

*

BY THEN, my garden was the subject of admiration from neighbors and passersby. It had become a shrine to Mother Nature and the place where I weeded out my sorrows by planting flower and herb seeds. I retreated to my backyard to grieve for my lost job and to obsess about the mole infestation that had taken over. Every day, I paced the garden slowly checking for new activity under the soil, and thought intensely on ways to exterminate them. The moles only multiplied.

With no current job, I had time to create a reliable writing routine and stick to it. I decorated an empty room with a corner desk, art, bookshelves, a coffee table, and an armchair. The room had a floor to ceiling window facing east, which allowed for plenty of sunlight and a view of the front garden. We painted the room a light green and completed the airy atmosphere with sheer curtains on the window.

After spending mornings gardening and battling moles, I sat in a wicker chair under the wisteria on the patio and concocted stories in my mind. Then I brewed a second cup of coffee and sat down to write. Stories flew from the tip of my fingers onto the screen. I knew little about writing or creating scenes or pacing. My stories came to life in sketches and character studies, but had little substance to hold them.

I found an adjunct faculty job at Tulsa Community College, and felt I finally had a job I loved. I had a small, reliable income, time and a beautiful space to write. But I still cringed with fear at the possibility of people looking at me through my laptop camera or hacking my computer files to create content on the web. I insisted on low medication doses and put greater effort into controlling my psychotic symptoms.

*

IN OWASSO, Jussef and I still struggled with unresolved marital issues. I couldn't change Jussef, his particular passive aggressiveness, and his obsessive thriftiness, his flirting with other women in public, or his mother, especially if I didn't attempt to change what was wrong with me. Neither could I excuse my violent behavior because of his flaws. He had to work on his problems, and I had to work on mine.

My most pressing issue was anger management. I couldn't control my emotions once an argument had passed the level of discussion. Every once in a while, I experimented with leaving the room and waiting until I had calmed down to approach the discussion from another perspective and another tone of voice. However, controlling my temper escaped me.

Jussef once told me that, when angry, my voice went from that of a little girl to a deep roar. In a way, that voice prevented anybody from coming near me, my way of protecting people from me. I threw and broke things, and I cussed both in Spanish and English. Then I cried abundantly, abused myself verbally, and rocked back and forth in an effort to comfort myself. I started dong these actions at an early age, from when my mother beat me. "You always do the same thing, like a pattern of behavior," Jussef said.

In therapy, I sat across the table in Dr. Hamilton's spacious office. On the right, French doors opened to a small patio with colorful plants. A kaleidoscope on the shelf behind me always tempted me to play with it, but I resisted. I never wanted to disrupt the conversation with any distractions. To my left, a chess board on a coffee table and a bonsai on the shelf. I enjoyed the serenity of this office with its sophisticated toys, its bright light, and organized atmosphere. There, I tried to convince my doctor that I didn't need any more medication because my husband was at fault.

"I was just trying to make my point when I lost control. I am sorry this is the second time I hit him."

"What would happen if you cut the drama, cut the flare, and tell him what's hurting you in a calm way?" asked Dr. Hamilton. With his white hair and old-fashioned courtesy, he now looked more like a father figure than a doctor.

While Jussef was at work, I sat alone in the studio I built in our home in Owasso. Here I wrote, read, and listened to music. I surrounded myself with art and books. I sat at my desk for hours, pondering the doctor's questions, thinking of what to do. I didn't want to be an abusive wife; I didn't want to justify my actions with Jussef's behavior either. What I did was wrong, and I had to change.

I left the safety of my studio and brewed some coffee. The aroma of the robust, black roast drip comforted me with the anticipation of a simple pleasure. With the warm cup of coffee in my hand, I opened the garden door and walked into my most personal space.

A robin's sudden flight rattled the leaves above my head. I sipped my coffee, sat in my garden chair, and listened. The birds showed me humanity in their complexity and beauty. The wrens chirped and chased each other like five year-old children playing soccer. The robins bullied anything they felt threatened their territory.

One good thing I would take from Oklahoma was that it forced me to be alone and still. Alienation was not a conscious choice, but I embraced it upon discovering that I couldn't relate to the people around me. Why waste time and energy in useless verbiage? What makes the Oklahoma Christians think that their delusion is more valid than mine?

Some ten years prior, in Ponca City, I walked into my backyard and hugged the silver maple standing twenty feet tall in a corner of the lot. Without family or god, solitude is infinite. As with any infinite space, I can fill my solitude any way my creativity sees fit. God died of shame and guilt when I was twelve, in the abusive home where I grew up.

From the pain of that alienation, I built a space that reflected my own spiritual needs, a shrine for Mother Nature. Wherever I went, I planted trees and flowers and created spaces for meditation and peace. In Owasso, I planted my third garden; it wouldn't be the last. Like that silver maple's, my roots didn't run deep.

Three wisterias intertwined around the arbor of my patio produced a much-needed respite from the plains' heat, and provided a safe habitat for birds. Underneath the arbor, the flowerbeds satisfied my creative cravings. I edged the beds with local limestone rocks and a dried creek. The beds burst with flowering or colorful perennials: hostas, liriopes, ferns, astilbe, Easter lilies, columbines, and coral-bells. I planted succulents in the shade. Lamb ears, day lilies, mums, hibiscus, cana-lilies, Indian blankets, and scabiosa went in the sun. I didn't want more vegetable or roses in my garden: vegetables produce work, and roses hurt.

Instead, thyme, parsley, oregano, mint, rosemary, coriander, chives, basil, and lavender perfumed my hands and my kitchen with their sweet gifts.

Seen from afar, it looked like an obsession, this weeding that I did one hour every day. On padded knees, I dug the crab grasses and threw them in a bucket, wiping the sweat from my forehead, swatting flies, mosquitoes, and the voice in my head, my mother's voice always bullying, harassing, humiliating. When I tired, I collected and cleaned the tools, put them back in place, and threw away the garden waste in the compost tumbler.

After I cleaned and aerated the soil, I always sat again for a few more minutes, for a moment of rumination. Other people called it prayer, but I was long since done with prayer. I reflected on my actions. I pondered on how to live my best life and how I could give back what had been bestowed on me. Those were the seeds I planted in my clean soul.

I built myself another family with my husband and two sons. I raised my children, and then opened the front door and windows so they could fly away free. They can come home to my embrace any time they want, but their lives fill their needs now without the omniscient presence of their mother. This family is all I have. It is my responsibility to maintain its integrity; I can't wreck it with my drama.

The doctor's question kept playing in my mind. *What will happen if you cut the drama, if you cut the flare*? In the garden, I kneeled down to weed dandelions, and cried when I realized how wrong I had been. *You are a drama queen. If you need drama to have an exciting life, join the local community theater, and cut the crap now. Avoid toxic people –gossipmongers- because they create drama and enjoy it. Avoid them like the plague, because it is you who's left with the medication and the apologies.*

Then I came up with a plan of action.

Because I had always expressed myself better in writing, I decided to write about what made me angry with Jussef. I then practiced my speech several times because I didn't want to choke up with emotion. When he got home that night, I gave him an earful of his deeds. I still cried and raised my voice, but I didn't break any dishes and definitely didn't try to hit him.

He listened to me when I said, "I am ready to divorce if that's what it takes."

One day he came to me and said, "Sorry, I have not been the best husband lately," and that's all I needed to forgive him. We hugged and cried and forgave each other. We gave our marriage a second chance.

Since that moment, I understood that I could achieve more with my words than with the flare of drama. I started practicing my particular form of meditation, which included gardening combined with soul searching. I consciously revisited my actions and reactions and considered ways in which I could become a better person. I learned that having a mental condition didn't mean I had to live in a crisis all the time. My quality of life has improved a great deal since I left the drama behind.

Mother Myth

I WANTED TO BREAK from my past in a healthy way, and writing was my tool. I had been writing all my life, but never attempted to publish or share my writing with others. Apart from establishing a writing routine to create without interruption, my small income as an adjunct faculty allowed me to attend conferences to hear published writers speak about their experiences. I also read memoirs with themes similar to mine (abuse and mental illness) to learn from them how to use writing to heal the wounds of the past, how to separate the facts from the magnified fears first birthed in my mind as a child. From *An Unquiet Mind* by Kay Redfield Jamison[4], I learned that one could achieve a well-rounded and productive life despite suffering from a mental disorder.

The Memory Palace[5] by Mira Bartók is a fascinating story about a woman who loses her memory as a consequence of a head trauma. Bartók is the daughter of a music prodigy who had an onset of schizophrenia on the day the Americans dropped one of their bombs on Japan. This extraordinarily gifted genius spiraled into madness, dragging her two young daughters with her. Like many children of the mentally ill, they developed the skills necessary to survive

---

[4] Redfield Jamison, Kay. *An Unquiet Mind: A Memoir of Moods and Madness. Vintage Books, 1997.*

[5] Bartok, Mira. The Memory Palace. Simon & Schuster. 2011.

the chaos of their lives. As young women trying to make it on their own, they found it more and more difficult to cope with their mother's breakdowns, threats, and bizarre life. They made a decision that would define the rest of their lives: they abandoned their mother.

I did not see this book as a "mea culpa" tale trying to validate a hard decision. Rather this story brought me to the realization that without a strong support system, children of the mentally ill will eventually turn their backs on their loved ones, feeding the urban environment with the soulless faces of the homeless. The book spoke also about reconciliation and forgiveness, about understanding and embracing one's flaws, and about life-saving decisions. It's a tale of compassion and empathy for the brilliant minds behind some homeless faces.

Inevitably, *Memory Palace* brought back memories of my own childhood. It wasn't that I didn't remember. My problem is that I remember too much. I remembered disturbing scenes of a madwoman blading a knife to her daughter and threatening to burn down her bedroom. My sister told me, "She didn't really mean to do those things." What my sister didn't or couldn't understand was that those acts of violence made an indelible mark on my psyche, and now I battled organizing, cleaning, and grooming obsessions because deep in my mind, I feared somebody would set fire to my room or smack my head against a wall.

Physical abuse, whether tangible or in the form of a threat, damages the psyche of the child who experiences it. I admired Bartók for forgiving her mother. I couldn't forgive mine.

*

ON HIGHWAY 60, I drove from Owasso to Ponca City every two months to meet Dr. Hamilton in his office. I couldn't find a therapist I liked or felt comfortable with in Tulsa, so I drove the 90 miles through The Plains for medication management and talk therapy.

"How are you going to honor Zoë's memory?" Dr. Hamilton asked again in his Ponca City office.

"I have to live to the best of my abilities," I said.

"The best of you is not in the past, Lisbeth," Dr. Hamilton said. "Strive to develop all you can be. "

The four hour round trip across the low hills of the Osage County with its austere landscape of tall grasses, oil pumps, and grazing angus, provided me with ample mental space for reflection on what had been discussed in therapy. Sometimes, on my way back, I turned left in Pawhuska and followed the 15 miles of country road to the Tall Grass Prairie Reserve, where herds of buffalo roamed free. Alone, I hiked for about an hour, taking in the immensity of the ochre ocean of grasses in front of my eyes. With my hiking boots stomping the ground firmly, I walked along the beaten path, stopping only to watch the deer run wild or to listen to the birds: blue jays, cardinals, and woodpeckers. Then, I followed my steps back to the car and continued to travel east to my suburban house, to my family and to my sheltered life.

Even the serenity of those bimonthly escapes was not enough to help me break from the past. I had held onto it for too long and needed a healthy outlet to deal with it.

"What happened to the book you were writing?" Dr. Hamilton asked. All his hair had turned white, and I wondered if he was close to retiring, if that meant I had to start looking for another psychiatrist.

"I told you I lost it. I don't know how to start again. I mean I have a hard copy, but it doesn't sound good to me anymore," I said.

"Start again," he said, encouraging me to continue writing the book I had drafted to honor Zoë.

I discarded the rough pages I'd previously written and started again from scratch, not without first sending a silent curse to the person who had found my flash drive and never returned it.

Soon, our sessions were not enough to deal with everything that the writing revealed. In my journal, I kept pouring out the trauma of my childhood. Out went the years of emotional and physical abuse perpetuated by my mother, the bullying by my siblings, the incest, the pain and shame, the scar on my face, and the phobia of cockroaches. Painful as they were, the memories came to life on paper and were exorcised by the power of writing. I started sending stories from my journal to my psychiatrist a week or so before our meetings, so he had time to prepare.

I wrote about the difference between having cancer and suffering from a mental disorder. Psychosis is not a death sentence, but it has the potential to kill me. Zoë had to stop the outpour of support she got after her diagnosis. On the other hand, the only support I had during my first psychotic episode in Canada was Zoë and Jussef. My mother believed I was manipulating my husband, and not one of my six siblings ever called to ask how I was doing. Jussef, Zoë, and my children were the only ones to pull me up when the demons in my mind came loose.

The unsent letters I had written to Zoë expanded into the outline of the book, with one or two fully developed chapters on my symptoms and treatment. I wanted to pay tribute to Zoë, to honor her for all she did for me, but I had no idea how to write a book. Until then, writing was something I did in my spare time, like crocheting and gardening.

I also began writing short stories. Writing brought back a great deal of pain, and without my friend present any longer, I didn't know what to do with it. Crafting stories about madness and dysfunctional families released some of that pain. Gardening and crocheting also provided a break from the memories.

After crocheting for an hour, I would sit down at the computer and pound out the memories and the long overdue catharsis of the child victim grown adult.

Then in 2012, I faced my greatest fear and set the goal to become a published writer. Pouring my pain into the garden and into the cathartic pages of my journal was no longer enough.

There was a little problem, though. I was afraid of media in any form. I was particularly afraid of communicating with people whose faces I couldn't see. What if "they" read my scribbling? What if "they" used social media to slander me, mock me, or accuse me of something I hadn't done? – I feared "they" were still out to get me.

I opened a blog account on wattpad.com, a Canadian website for readers and writers, sort of like a big writing critique group with millions of followers.

Wattpad required a registered membership. Posting there didn't make my work fully public, and I felt protected. I posted my first story on wattpad.com under the penname Cayena. The feedback was positive and encouraging, but I felt isolated and detached from the other writers I had never seen.

I knew I was far from calling myself a writer, but I had taken the first step in the right direction and could only move forward from there on. Poems soon followed, and by January 2013, I was posting weekly.

At this time, I also asked Doctor Hamilton for a supervised break from medication. I worked better without meds because I was able to feel the rush of creativity in a natural way. It was a risky decision, but it was worth it. I saved every penny I had earned as an adjunct faculty to pay for writing classes online and to attend conferences.

For years, I felt crippled by the ideation of being under constant surveillance. Medication and treatment, the love of my family, and my best warrior effort to be the best person I could be didn't stop the fear of being watched.

After many weeded dandelions though, I came up with this: I couldn't get rid of the feeling of being under a watchful eye, but I knew it didn't kill me to live with it. "They" could monitor me all "they" wanted, but "they" couldn't affect my life in anyway. I needed to learn to live with the fear and overcome it. I also began putting a piece of paper over the laptop camera before I got to work.

For spring break 2013, I gave myself the best present I had received in years - a weeklong writing retreat in the Cascade Mountains of Washington State. Two time zones away from home, with a group of people completely unknown to me, alone and without medication for the first time in fifteen years, I attended the Wild Mountain Writing Retreat, organized by Theo Nestor. There I met real writers, mostly women who had overcome their own obstacles. The event gave me a much-needed new group of friends with similar interests in writing, and a network of writers across the states.

In Theo Nestor's workshops, and later in Ariel Gores Literary Kitchen (from Oakland, CA) online, I learned to give my work a much-needed sense of urgency. Without it, I ran the risk of losing pages again in the next relocation.

*

DESPITE ALL THE PROGRESS I'd made trying to live a happy life, I still could feel the weight of something big dragging me down.

The secrets of a survivor are such that we keep it even from ourselves.

I feared dealing with my past would break me down, revert my psyche to square one, and send me to a point where I would need somebody to put the medication in my mouth.

Coming out and telling the truth meant telling myself what laid so heavy on my heart, and recognizing it as the venom which had almost destroyed my life, the reason for my self-destruction and dissociation, an ugly event so loaded with the dark side of motherhood that even a victim-child couldn't open her eyes to see it.

We don't really know why a mind decides to speak at any specific moment. In December 2013, I attended a writing workshop organized by Theo Nestor in Santa Fe, New Mexico. I took a seat on the right side of the room, in one of the middle rows, next to other writers I had met the previous evening. The tall adobe walls and the vaulted ceilings gave the space an air of a Spanish cathedral, a magnificent place to hear sacred truths and receive blessings, except I wasn't a religious person. I was there to hear my powerful truth with the blessing of my teachers and peers, other memoirists like me, who had all previously walked the road of exorcising pain from their souls with a keyboard as a tool.

With my bottle of water, and my perfectly sharpened pencils, I sat there nodding and taking notes as the faculty asked poignant questions and suggested writing exercises. It was an exciting day with Natalie Goldberg and Julia Cameron as feature speakers. I was prepared for magic to happen.

Theo Nestor directed us to jot down five things we didn't dare to say aloud. PUM! It hit me, I wasn't looking for it, not at that moment, not in front of all those people, but it did, and I am glad. My hand ran swiftly on the three hole punched lined paper as I wrote, "The Mother Myth." I underlined those words with two firm strokes. "We don't want to speak the truth against the mother," I continued, "because it's easier to accept the idea that mothers mean no harm and deserve forgiveness. I forgive you not, mother. You are a feeble old woman now, thousands of miles away, but you are as guilty of IT now as you were then. You are the cockroach in my closet."

The workshop continued all day. I heard my writing heroes speak, and I did a walking meditation conducted by Natalie Goldberg. That put me in the right place and state of mind to continue what had just started. At the end of the day, I retired to my room, sat at the desk, and continued where I had left off.

I wrote for two hours straight about my mother: how she had destroyed every particle of my self esteem, how she had caused irreparable damage to my mind, how at fourteen she had *attempted* to find out if I was still a virgin.

After I finished, I put the pencil down and cried. I had finally realized why it was impossible for me to forgive. Mothers are capable of perverse acts, and it's okay if I don't forgive mine now that I am also an adult woman. She was never neglectful; she was an abuser. I have a moral responsibility to the parent who fed me three times a day, paid for my education, and always saw that I had clean clothes to wear, but I couldn't forgive my mother for the twenty-three years of physical and emotional abuse she inflicted on me.

In my last months of therapy, I finally understood that my unresolved childhood issues continue to be determining factors and causes for my feelings of hopelessness. I realized it was these issues that had once made me suicidal.

It has been scientifically proven that the pervasive exposure to adverse events during childhood produces chemical reactions in the body and cardiac responses, resulting in a number of physical and mental ailments, hence the name Toxic Stress.

In her TED Talk[6], Dr. Nadine Burke Harris[7] refers to a study by the Center for Disease Control[8] which concluded that "childhood exposure to trauma was strongly and scientifically linked to all kinds of ailments and risky behaviors: heart disease, hepatitis, autoimmune disease, cancer, chronic obstructive pulmonary disease, depression and suicide." Victims of child abuse

---

6 https://www.ted.com/talks/nadine_burke_harris_how_childhood_trauma_affects_health_across_a_lifetime

7 http://www.tedmed.com/speakers/show?id=293067

8 https://www.cdc.gov/

are 4.5 times more likely to develop depression and 12 times more likely to attempt against their own life than their healthy counterparts. [9]

Harris stresses the use of the right tools to develop a public health campaign focused on the prevention of childhood trauma in whatever form it presents itself: physical, emotional or sexual abuse, neglect, dysfunctionality, addiction, extreme poverty, or mental illness in the home.

Like other diseases that affect the general population, childhood trauma doesn't know race or socio economic boundaries. It's everybody's problem, and its prevention should be treated as a public health issue, much like AIDS. Harris is leading a prevention movement that educates parents much in the way we educate them to prevent accidents in the home. I can state without a doubt that the trauma I experienced during the twenty-five years I lived in my parents' house led to the mental condition I suffer today as an adult.

Given the chance to stay in my life, my mother would have continued to abuse me. Much like the mother character in the book *Ena oj Eve*, by Ariel Gore[10]. The abuse of the main character doesn't end despite the fact that the mother is dying of lung cancer. But one thing I learned from that story is that humor, albeit dark makes for a strong survival tool. We have to smile all the time. We are all on candid camera.

*

ZOË AND MY MOTHER sit at opposite ends of the spectrum of motherhood. Zoë was nurturing and accepting, but I understand she was not my real mother. My real mother, on the contrary, is an unhappy woman that destroyed my self-esteem and denied me love as a child and moral support as a woman.

In order to stand on my own feet, conscious of my past but not governed by it, I must search inside me for my ideal mother, the mother I wished I had

[9] https://www.cdc.gov/violenceprevention/childmaltreatment/consequences.html
[10] Gore, Ariel. *The End of Eve*. Hawthorne Books. 2014.

and the mother I think I should be. That mother is within me. I must find her in order to let go of the pain.

Motherhood is at the core of my identity. I may not have been the perfect mother, but I learned to appreciate life for my children. Now I am proud to say that I stopped the cycle of abuse within my family.

I suffer from a terrible disease, but thanks to an extraordinary friendship, the healing power of love, and my determination to overcome obstacles, I live a healthy life. Although at times, it feels like I have a broken wing, I am no longer the victim of my circumstances. As long as writing continues to be a part of my life, and I can plant trees and flowers to make this a better world, I will fly free of the crippling effects of abuse. Though the memories will stay with me the rest of my life, I am a good mother, a passionate lover, a loyal friend, and I am happy with myself.

The Sound of Home

SIRENS ARE THE SOUNDS I now associate with our home in Palos Verdes, California, after an accident almost took my life some fourteen months ago.

I was driving through an intersection when a silver sports car slammed against my green Ford Fiesta, the one I bought with Zoë's gift. On contact, my car spun like a carousel, and I felt like I was riding a green mare. On the first spin, I saw the silver car and the driver, a white man. Then trees and the color blue, like the ocean that day. I heard screams, too, not mine. Then I saw death winking her eye to me and holding me in a long suffocating embrace.

I pushed the red button and escaped her cold arms. Head first.

I surfaced through a narrow passage I opened with my feet, through pain and confusion, out to a bright day and much gratitude.

"I am the daughter of a green mare," I thought.

"She's out. She can't walk. Call 911," a voice screamed triumphantly, happy to see me alive. He held me in his warm arms, and I cried.

People rushed from their cars and picked me up from the hot asphalt.

"You made it. You are alive. Thank God you are alive," a man with a Spanish accent said as he grabbed my ankles.

Another man held me from under my armpits. They placed me on the curb in the shade of a small tree. I saw my car on the opposite side of the road, wheels up, a mangle of green metal. Broken glass was everywhere. Black auto parts lay scattered on the side of the road.

Somebody spoke from the inside of my car. "Are you hurt?" The automatic emergency system had called 911. My car alarm blared with deafening urgency.

"Please, call my husband," I said to no one in particular.

"What's the telephone number?" a male voice asked.

"I don't know. Do you know what happened?" My voice sounded away.

"Do you have a phone?" asked somebody else.

"It's in the car. There. You see?" I pointed at the rear window. The telephone seemed suspended from the broken glass.

"It's inside the car. I got it," another man yelled.

"El carro está al revés, mi amor."

"She is saying the car is upside down" a Latino man translated for the others.

"¿Qué? ¿Dónde estás?" Jussef asked on the phone.

"Cerca de la casa." I knew I was near home, but I didn't know the address. I had just moved here a month ago. A fire truck, approaching, didn't let me hear Jussef.

A female firefighter squatted in front of me. First she looked at me holding my hands to my ears. She turned back and yelled to nobody in particular, "Can somebody turn the car alarm off, please?"

"Ma'am, do you know what happened?" I asked.

"What's your name? I'm gonna place this around your neck," she said.

My tears pooled at the edge of the neck collar. "Lisbeth."

"How old are you?"

"50."

"Where are you?"

"In California. I just moved here from Oklahoma."

"Any medical conditions?"

"I am mentally ill."

I survived the accident with only bruises on my body and the strong conviction that I have something to do on this earth or else I wouldn't have come out alive from the mangle of metal with the wheels up on the opposite side of the road.

In my condo in Palos Verdes, I take one corner of my blanket and slide it across my body; then I pull my feet over the bed and onto the carpeted floor. I stand up and turn to look at the day through the northwest facing window of my room. The blue of the sea fills the rectangular view, but not its roar. It's the sirens I hear.

Every house I have lived in has had a particular sound.

In Caracas, frequent shootings broke out at all hours of the day, but especially during the night, when muggers terrorized those coming back late from work in the alley behind the building where we used to live. The heavy traffic noise didn't reach us because we lived in the north side, looking at El Avila. From time to time, a scandalous choir of macaws flew to our balcony to delight us with their show.

Our first house in Canada, the one we bought on Dunnview Court after three years of renting roach-infested apartments, filled daily with the sounds of young children coming in and out with their little mudded feet, their contagious laughter, and annoying shrills. We never saw them again, the children we left behind in haste when my husband received an "offer too good to resist."

I move away from the window and walk to the bathroom to brush my teeth, take a quick shower, and change into fresh, clean clothes. Downstairs, I set the coffee machine for three cups of the dark liquid: one for now, one for after lunch, one for mid afternoon. While I wait for the machine to cough out the coffee, I hope it will stir me awake, shake the pull that's tugging me down.

"Chill out, Lisbeth. It's coffee, not liquid happiness," I tell myself. The entire ritual tells me there is continuity despite the many changes, that everything remains the same, that I will be okay. Like the coffee I favor, I am a light roast, but full-bodied and robust.

I open the patio door and step onto the cold terracotta floor with my bare feet, feeling the warm air outside. A leaf blower cries loud somewhere in the neighborhood, predicting a morning without a visit from the hummingbirds. I have cleaned the rectangle of dirt in the patio and planted several drought resistant plants. It's beginning to look like a garden, but without the butterflies, or the songs of the jays and wrens, or the chirping of the robins that used to inhabit my garden in Oklahoma, the last casualty in this series of arrivals and farewells my life has turned into.

Inside my living room, the art on the walls reminds me of my homeland and its colors and sounds, its luscious vegetation, the spectacular landscape of a country gone wrong. I close my eyes, and I feel nostalgic. This longing for a place that was once familiar and vital to me now lives inside of me between the lungs and the heart, and feeds from my oxygen and my blood. I remember a place where the ocean water is warm and the vegetation green 365 days a year. I miss the sun over my head from eleven a.m. to four p.m. mahogany trees and orchids, politically incorrect humor, parties that last all night, and friends that pop up in my apartment unannounced looking for condoms as if in a weird Seinfeld episode.

I go to the kitchen, pour myself a glass of cold water and drink it slowly, allowing the liquid to moisten my dry throat. No, it never feels like home, this duplex apartment south of Los Angeles, with its uncomfortable constant indoor temperature of 65 F, its low ceiling, 70s style, and staggering mortgage.

Everything else about the city enchants me to the point of gratitude. During my sixteen months in LA, I have seen more movies than I saw the last twelve years of living in Oklahoma. I have met editors and fellow writers. I have gone to literary readings and joined a critique group (The South Bay Writing Group), which I meet with once a week. I have danced and attended concerts. I have eaten in splendid restaurants and at popular food trucks. I have hiked mountains and bathed in the cold waters of the Pacific Ocean. I've seen whales, dolphins, and seals in their natural habitat. I even read my poetry to fellow writers at Avenue 50 in Highland Park. Best of all, not one single person has invited me to Bible study.

I should be happy. Yet I am not.

A feeling of doom hovers over me, like the hummingbird that comes to my window when I sit down to crochet in a corner of my living room.

"Maybe I don't want to feel happy. Maybe I resist accepting that I can be happy anywhere I go," I tell myself.

"Probably the issue is fear," I reason as though in a conversation with myself, "fear to feel comfortable again, to feel at home, because whenever I start feeling comfortable somewhere I leave, and I don't want to leave. I want to stay here. I don't want to move again. I want to grow roots."

Like the maple tree I embraced some twelve years ago, my roots don't run deep. I will move again.

A job will soon take me to the Bay Area, where I will start a new life without my partner of twenty-eight years. I will be away from the scent of his body, from the sunsets we have watched together, from the hand that held me in my darkest hour, and from the tears I've cried since we moved to this place. I will start a new life away from him, from my friend and lover.

I want to say goodbye to the Venezuelan friends I've met in the last months here, and to the children I will not see grow, like so many others we've left behind, but I can't let Jussef know that I already contacted a family and divorce lawyer and paid the retainer with the joint account. I decided on a pool party. He does not agree, but I do it anyway.

I enjoy the day, watching the children have fun in the condo pool, sharing shawarmas and beers with the adults, while Jussef flirts with the youngest woman in the group. I also flirt with him, trying not to give any indication of my anger and disappointment. So many women have come between us, invited by him, in ever more daring stunts of deceit.

"Too many to count," he said after he decided to come clean about his philandering.

The party moves from the clubhouse to our house, where we have coffee and chat some more. When they leave, I'm ready.

"Please, sit down. I need to talk to you," I say.

"Uh, Oh."

"Tomorrow you will receive an email from a lawyer. I filed for divorce last Friday. I will move to Oakland on October 21st," I say, my eyes fixed on his, waiting for his reaction to make my next move.

His nostrils flare up, his thick eyebrows meet at the center. "How are you going to pay for a lawyer?" he asks.

"I already did. I paid with the joint checking account," I say.

He rubs his eyes with the palm of his hands, and then slides the hands past his eyebrows and over his balding head. "You can't use that money. I worked for that."

"Sorry to break it to you, but that's also my money," I reply.

"I told you not to do a pool party, and you did. I told you not to throw a lawyer at me, and you did. I told you not to use the checking account for a lawyer, and you did. What's happening to you? ¿Te volviste loca?" He continues raising his voice, standing up from the chair, tracing his hands over his balding head, and pacing around the room in spastic moves. "I raised your child. I pulled you from the ground. My mother always told me you would sharpen your nails. She was right."

"I am slow. It took me twenty-eight years to sharpen my nails," I say, wiping the tears from my face.

"What would Zoë say? She wouldn't agree to this."

"Zoë didn't want me to live in a toxic relationship without respect or dignity. She wanted the best for me," I say.

The perks I have enjoyed as a corporate wife will dissipate like the purple bloom of the jacaranda tree in late June, with a mess at the feet that reminds us of its former splendor. Now a woman in my 50s, I must carry on alone, using the skills I have learned to deal with the crisis and upheavals of my mental condition. I must start again at zero, putting one foot in front of the other, waiting for my opportunity, and working hard to regain a financial and professional footing in this world. It'll be hard, but I've been through hell and back before and came out stronger. Besides, I don't have anything else to lose. I already lost my best friend, my mind, and the love of my life. With a box loaded with tools for coping with bipolar disorder and psychosis, with my children grown into wonderful human beings, with the certainty that even on the gloomiest day life is worth living, every second of it, I start this next chapter of my life on my feet and on my own terms.

Wherever I go, and whatever I do, I will carry with me the images, the colors, the scents, and the sounds of this home, together with all the homes I have left behind. I will always carry with me the sound of his heartbeat against my ear when I rested on his chest, exhausted from lovemaking. The sound of home.

Oakland, January 2016.

Aruba
Barbados
Curaçao
Grenada
Barranquilla
Maracaibo
Caracas
Trinidad
and Tobago
Cartagena
Barquisimeto
Valencia
Panama City
Bucaramanga
Venezuela
Georgetown
Medellín
Paramaribo
Bogotá
Pereira
Guyana
Cali
Colombia
Suriname
Boa Vista
STATE OF
RORAIMA
Quito
Map data ©2017 Google, INEGI

About the Author

Lisbeth Coiman is a bilingual writer wandering the immigration path from Venezuela to Canada, to the US. She has performed any available job from maid to college administrator. Her work has been published in HipMama, YAY LA, and Nailed Magazine, and featured in the Listen to Your Mother Show in 2015.

In her bilingual blog, www.lisbethcoiman.com, she muses about living with a serious mental disorder. She dances salsa to beat depression.